A GREAT WEEKEND IN

NEW YORK

New York

a city of contrasts

September 11th 2001 is imprinted on the minds of every New Yorker, indeed every citizen of America and the rest of the world. It changed the skyline of New York, the face of international politics and the course of history. However, New Yorkers are a resilient bunch and the words of former mayor, Rudy Guiliani, still resound today: 'Tomorrow, New York is going to be here. And we're going to rebuild, and we're going to be stronger than we were before.' Defining New York is not easy. In the opening frames of *Manhattan*, Woody Allen tries in vain to define New York, finally allowing Gershwin's *Rhapsody in Blue* to take over. New York is a mercurial and fascinating city, the gateway to what is still the 'promised land' for thousands of people. Watched over by the Statue of Liberty, it has become a global crossroads, a vast jumble of people and places. You have to take several bites out of the Big Apple to discover the full flavour of its districts – the bohemian West Village, SoHo with its galleries, trendy TriBeCa and Downtown with its bankers and Masters of the Universe.

Cross the street, and you'll find you've moved from luxury apartment blocks to barren wasteland and from one ambiance to another. Like a giant living organism, New York is endlessly changing, moving, renewing itself, being built and disappearing. Little by little, luxury lofts take the place of warehouses and fashionable districts migrate from place to place, giving New York its elusive, mobile character.

The multitude of little villages that make up the microcosm are all quite different. Here, we have Asia and all the smells of the orient, Peking duck in the shop windows and a McDonald's sign adorned with Chinese characters. Over there, we have Little Italy and a taste of the Mediterranean, with terrace restaurants and the aroma of pizza and cappucino. Small Korean grocery stores compete for

preferably on glamorous 5th Avenue, arguably the most famous street in the world. New York has the finest department stores in the country, as well as a multitude of trendy boutiques and stalls. Every district has its speciality but all are Aladdin's caves full of treasures waiting

business all over the city, while West Indian newspaper sellers keep watch from their stalls.

Living side by side in the metropolis are people of every race, culture and creed. Whatever their origins, they've come together in this melting pot to make the city the capital of a continent and perhaps the entire world. The creative vibe in New York is strong and there is a buzz that is found in no other US city. The eclectic mix of people and cultures provides an ideal platform for new ideas, new fashions, art,

to be discovered. With all kinds of electronic equipment, CDs, cameras, sportswear, fashion accessories, art reproductions and household goods on offer

caught up in the whirlwind of bars in the trendier districts. Remember that this is the 'city that never sleeps' – it won't give you any respite.

Beneath the apparent rationality of streets laid out on a grid pattern lies a poetry that has never ceased to fascinate film-makers from Martin Scorsese to John Cassavetes by way of perhaps the city's most ardent admirer, Woody Allen. You, too, will feel it when the sun glints on the steel and glass of the skyscrapers and the city buzzes and rumbles to life on the first morning of your stay in the most exciting city in the world.

writing and poetry. There is always something new and exciting to uncover, and the most curious and exotic styles come and go.

Now more than ever, New York is at the forefront of fashion, responsible for starting the most avant-garde trends. All the well-known couturiers have shops here,

at sometimes laughable prices, this is a shopping paradise.

When evening comes, how else will you end the day but by going to a fashionable club, listening to jazz or seeing a musical on Broadway. Be dazzled by the bright lights of Times Square, which have crystallised the dreams of so many Americans, or get

How to get there

There's always something going on in the Big Apple and whatever time of year you choose, the shopping is always great! Just bear in mind that it can be stiflingly hot in the summer and bitterly cold in January and February – after all, Canada isn't that far away.

WHEN SHOULD YOU GO?

New Yorkers young and old alike simply adore carnivals, festivals and parades of every kind. Throughout the year, from late spring to the depths of winter, the festival calendar is full and you'll find no lack of reasons to spend a few days in New York. For more precise information about specific events contact NYC's Official Visitor Information Center, 810 7th Avenue, ☎ 1 800 692 84 74 (freephone) or ☎ 484 12 22 (open Mon.-Fri. 8.30am-6pm, Sat., Sun. and public hols. 9am-5pm). They also have a very useful website: www.nycvisit.com

SPRING

The best time to spend a few days in New York is in the spring or autumn. From mid-March it's pleasantly cool and invigorating, and with the temperature starting to rise and the first street parades taking place, you can tell that summer is on its way. The famous St Patrick's Day Parade on 17 March, the Irish national holiday, is certainly worth going out of your way for, and you could well find yourself in a pub at the end of the day. Later in the month, on 25 March, comes Greek Independence Day. On Easter Sunday, the spectacular Easter Day Parade takes place, with its outrageous costumes. Easter also marks the opening of the baseball season, which continues until October.

SUMMER

By the time June arrives, the weather is much hotter and you can watch the Puerto Rican Day Parade and, on the last Sunday in June, the unmissable Gay and Lesbian Pride Parade (information: ☎ 807 74 33). This colourful procession makes its way through the streets of Midtown to Greenwich Village and is something no self-respecting, trendy New Yorker would dream of missing. July and August are possibly the most trying months of the year. Temperatures can soar as high as 40°C/100°F and can make life in the city quite unbearable. At such times, air-conditioned shops and restaurants are the only pleasant places to be. In late June or early July, jazz fans can enjoy the world-famous JVC Jazz Festival (for concert information: ☎ 501 13 90), with two weeks of live performances by the greatest jazz musicians in the world. In mid July the famous Central Park Summerstage is held (information: ☎ 360 27 77). Every weekend in June until the end of August, internationally-renowned musicians play free concerts

TRAVELLING ACROSS THE POND

Because of the time difference, most flights leave Europe in the late morning and arrive in the US around 8-8.30am, or by mid-afternoon at the latest. The journey isn't too arduous. By the time you've had lunch, watched a film, had a little nap or read for a while, you're there. You'll still have the late afternoon and evening to recover and unpack. Try to stay awake until 9 or 10pm (i.e. 4am European time). It makes for a long day, but you'll sleep through the night and wake up feeling relaxed and refreshed, ready to start exploring the city without wasting any time. If you're worried about developing DVT (deep vein thrombosis) during your flight, drink plenty of water and try some foot exercises, such as rotating your ankles and wriggling your toes. Those with a higher risk factor (such as pregnant women or those who are overweight) should consider wearing compression stockings. On the way back, the flights leave the US late at night and arrive back in Europe early the next day, which means it's important to get a few hours sleep if you don't want to develop jet-lag. Earplugs and drinking lots of water rather than alcohol should help.

in the park. Blues, jazz, world music, reggae — all styles of music are represented. In late August-early September (information: ☎ (718) 760 62 00), tennis fans can take their seats for the US Open and swelter as they enjoy the rhythm of the game on the terraces of Flushing Meadows.

AUTUMN

Autumn lends the city a special charm — the temperature is mild and the light is beautiful. In early September, the West Indian Day Carnival (information: ☎ (718) 625 15 15) takes place in Brooklyn. The city's Italian community celebrates San Gennaro's Day in the third week of September on Mulberry Street. This is followed by the Polish community's festival, the Pulaski Day Parade, which is held in early October. Halloween falls on 31 October and is widely celebrated, with New Yorkers donning all manner of strange disguises. The parade starts in SoHo at 7pm (information: ☎ 475 33 33 ext. 7787). The city is transformed as if by magic as the streets fill with witches and fairies and you'll see plenty to make you shudder by the light of the pumpkin lanterns. This is also the time of the New York marathon, a race no self-respecting runner would dream of missing. The event attracts a vast field of competitors (around 30,000 a year) for the 26 mile race ending in Central Park (information: ☎ 860 44 55). Finally, the Thanksgiving Parade sponsored by Macy's department store takes place in late November, with decorated floats thronging the streets and a multitude of Father Christmases (information: ☎ 888 692 870, website: www.nycvp.com).

WINTER

New York winters are generally severe, with the temperature often falling below zero and a dry, biting wind from Labrador to keep people from lingering on the streets. The Christmas period can nevertheless be a good time to visit the city. The atmosphere is truly magical and Americans come from all over the country to see the sparkling window displays. With the city brilliantly lit, everyone gets into the festive spirit. The Christmas Tree Lighting Ceremony, which takes place in early December, is an unforgettable event. Decorated with over 4 miles of fairy lights, the giant fir tree standing in the Rockefeller Center is like something out of a fairy-tale.

Early February, can be a good time of year for sports lovers to visit the city. This is when the hardy can join in the ascent of the 86 floors of the Empire State Building. With more than 1,575 steps to climb from the ground to the 86th floor, the current record stands at 12 minutes (Empire State Building Run-up, information: ☎ 860 44 55).

HOW TO GET THERE

FROM THE UK

Many major airlines offer flights to New York JFK or Newark airports. Both are about a half hour bus or taxi ride from the centre of Manhattan. It's worth checking airline websites for cheap offers. Some airlines which have direct flights from London include:

British Airways
☎ 0845 77 333 77
www.ba.com
Flies direct from London Heathrow to New York JFK and Newark airports.

CUSTOMS AND IMMIGRATION

Importing live organic matter, such as plants or certain cheeses, into the US is strictly forbidden. Meat, both raw and cooked, vegetables, furs and the skins of endangered species are also prohibited. However, you can import a litre of wine or alcohol (if you're over 21) and 200 cigarettes, 50 cigars or 2kg (4.4lbs) of tobacco duty free. Any gifts you bring must not exceed a total value of $100, or you'll have to pay 10% tax. Gifts may include 100 cigars with gift exemption, but no alcohol. Cuban cigars are banned. Goods worth more than $100 should be entered on the form you'll be given on the plane. If you're having any special medical treatment, carry the prescription for your medicines. If prohibited substances are found when your luggage is searched (and the search can be extremely thorough), expect to have them confiscated on the spot – customs officers are not well known for their sense of humour.
When you arrive in New York, you'll find that immigration is no mere formality. You may be asked searching questions about the reasons for your visit. If you have difficulty remembering the address of your hotel, keep it on you. You may need it to prove your visit is bona fide if you want to avoid finding yourself on the next plane back.

Virgin Atlantic
☎ (01293) 511 581
www.virgin-atlantic.com
Flies direct from London Heathrow to New York JFK and Newark airports. Often offers good deals, particularly off-season.

Continental
☎ 0800 776 464

www.continental.com
Flies direct from London
Heathrow and Gatwick to
New York JFK and Newark.

FROM IRELAND
Aerlingus offers direct flights
to New York, but it may be
cheaper to fly with another
airline via London.

Aerlingus
☎ 0818 365000
www.aerlingus.ie
Flights direct from Dublin
and Belfast to New York.

British Airways
☎ 1 800 626 747
www.ba.com
Flights to New York JFK and
Newark airports via the UK.

FROM AUSTRALIA AND NEW ZEALAND

Cathay Pacific
☎ 13 17 47 (Australia)
0508 800 454 (NZ)

www.cathaypacific.com
Flights daily from Sydney,
Melbourne and Auckland
via Hong Kong to New York
JFK.

Qantas
☎ 13 13 13 (Australia)
0800 808 767 (NZ)
www.qantas.com
Flies daily from Sydney and
Melbourne via Los Angeles to
New York JFK.

Singapore Airlines
☎ 131 011 (Australia)
☎ 0800 808 9090 (NZ)
www.singaporeair.com
Flies twice daily from Sydney,
Melbourne and Auckland via
Singapore to JFK and Newark.

FROM WITHIN THE USA
There are many domestic
airlines which offer flights
from all major US cities to
New York. These include:

CURRENCY

To foreign visitors American money can be confusing. The bills – whether one dollar or fifty dollars – are all the same size and colour, so be careful when paying!
The only way to tell them apart is by their portraits of great American politicians, as well as the number on the bill of course. The $1 bill portrays George Washington, the $5 bill Abraham Lincoln, $10 Alexander Hamilton, $20 Andrew Jackson, $50 Simpson Grant and finally the $100 bill shows Benjamin Franklin. Bills of $500 or $1,000 are fairly rare and taxi drivers in particular are not keen on being presented with bills for large amounts. Hang on to your $1 bills as they are handy for tipping. There are various coins, from the quarter (25 cents) and dime (10 cents) to the nickel (5 cents) and penny (1 cent).

Delta
☎ 1 800 2211 212
www.delta.com

US Airways
☎ 1 800 428 4322
www.usairways.com

United Airlines
☎ 1 800 241 6522
www.unitedairlines.com

American Airlines
1 800 433 7300
www.im.aa.com

FROM CANADA
Most American airlines offer regular flights from major Canadian cities.

BY BUS
Greyhound offers services from all over Canada to New York. For fares and schedules check out their website: www.greyhound.com or call ☎ 1 800 229 9424.

You can also check train times and prices at your local station or travel agent.

FROM THE AIRPORT TO THE CITY CENTRE
New York has three airports, JFK, Newark and La Guardia. All three are well connected to the city centre by various means of transport. Just follow the 'Ground Transportation' signs in the airport.

Arriving at JFK
When you've just had a long plane journey, you won't want to waste any time getting to your hotel. The easiest way to reach the city is by taxi and the trip to the centre of Manhattan will cost a flat fee of $35 (non-metered) plus bridge and tunnel tolls and tip. It will take anywhere from 30 minutes to an hour. Fixed

rates have been laid down to prevent unscrupulous drivers overcharging for the journey and these are rigorously enforced. Do, however, avoid unlicensed cabs, whose drivers often solicit customers around the baggage claim areas, and always take a Yellow Medallion cab. You could ride the subway for $1.50 but you'll have to wait for the free blue-and-yellow shuttle bus to take you to the Howard Beach JFK Airport station first. A weekly or monthly MetroCard allows you to travel on both the bus and the subway (see p. 30). The journey takes at least an hour as the queue can be pretty long. You can also go by bus or van services. These are cheaper than a taxi but take longer and won't drop you at the door of your hotel. From JFK the buses run by Express Shuttle USA will stop anywhere between 23rd and 125th Street for $14, while the NY Airport Service Express bus ☎ (718)

875 8200, takes between 45-60 minutes and stops at Grand Central Terminal, the Port Authority bus terminal and Penn Station.

Arriving in Newark
A taxi takes about 20-45 minutes and costs between $34-55 plus tolls and tip to reach the centre of Manhattan from the airport. To get to the city by subway, first take a 62 bus to the terminus, then the Path Train, which will take you to the heart of Manhattan. From Newark, the Express Shuttle USA buses will stop at the hotel of your choice for $14, but you can, if you prefer, catch an Olympia Airport Express bus which costs $11-16 to Midtown Manhattan and runs every 20-25 minutes. AirTrain Newark is the new regional rail connection from all three terminals into Penn Station at 7th Avenue and 33rd Street in Manhattan. It takes 45-60 minutes and costs $11.15.

Arriving at La Guardia
The 20-40 minute taxi ride to the centre of Manhattan from

La Guardia Airport will cost you around $16-26. However, if you want to travel more cheaply, you can take an Express Shuttle USA or a NY Airport Service Express bus for around $13. the M60 bus costs $1.50 and drops you in Uptown Manhattan from where you can join the subway.

FORMALITIES

Under the new visa waiver programme, visitors from the UK, Ireland, Australia and New Zealand only need a valid passport and proof of return (i.e. return air ticket) to enter the USA. Canadians only need proof of citizenship. If you plan to stay for longer than 90 days you'll require a visa, for which you should contact your local US Consulate.

IDENTITY CARD

If you want to drive in the USA, you must have held a driving licence for over a year. It's a good idea to take your licence anyway, as you'll find it an invaluable source of ID, particularly when trying to get into bars and clubs where

the bouncers can be very strict about checking customers are over 21.

HEALTH AND INSURANCE

Being ill in the USA is best avoided, as the cost of medical care is exorbitant. To avoid unpleasant surprises, it's advisable to take out comprehensive travel insurance before travelling to New York. However, check what's covered by your homeowners' insurance first, as this sometimes covers theft during travel. Your travel agent will be able to arrange cover, otherwise contact an insurance company direct. **The Travel Insurance Agency** is based in the UK (☎ 020 8446 5414, www.travelinsurers.com) but covers non-UK residents at no extra premium. Alternatively, try **Worldwide Travel Insurance** (01892 83 33 38, www.worldinsure.com).

Canadians are covered by their home province's health insurance plan for up to 90 days after leaving the country.

In Australia contact the **Australian Federation of Travel Agents** on ☎ 02 9264 3299 (Sydney) or www.afta.com.au

USEFUL WEBSITES

www.ny.com
www.newyork.citysearch.com
www.nycvisit.com
These websites are packed with tips and information for visitors and are well worth a visit.

A VERTICAL CITY

In a constant search for room to expand and grow, New York has ceaselessly built taller, more functional skyscrapers – steel and glass structures, born of close cooperation between architects and engineers, art and technology, that are monuments to our times. Following the events of September 11th, the Empire State building is once more the city's tallest edifice.

building's restrained Classicism gave way to more ornate structures that took their inspiration from Antiquity and the Gothic buildings of Europe.

THE ORIGINS OF AMERICAN SKYSCRAPERS

Skyscrapers first appeared on the scene around 1880 in New York and Chicago, the two largest urban centres in America at that time. In the aftermath of the bloody Civil War, the already dynamic and prosperous cities of the northeast and midwest began to grow at a dizzying rate following the influx of newcomers to the region. With the invention of the elevator and steel frames which facilitated lighter buildings, skyscrapers were henceforth free to reach for the sky.

THE FIRST BUILDINGS – CLASSIC AND HISTORICAL INSPIRATION

The turn of the century saw the construction of impressive tower blocks, such as the Fuller Building (or Flatiron), a majestic column built by Burnham in 1902 on the corner of 5th Avenue and Broadway. In the early years of the 20th century, this

THE TRIUMPH OF ART DECO

The 1920s saw a boom in the construction industry and the triumph of Art Deco, which

lent the new skyscrapers a more striking elegance. New York transposed the rhythms and colours of jazz into its architecture, and skyscrapers were decorated with deliberately symmetrical patterns. One of the finest new buildings of the time, the

Chrysler Building, built between 1928 and 1930, is entirely covered in stainless steel plates.

THE INTERNATIONAL STYLE

After World War II, skyscrapers began to spring up everywhere. The materials used – steel, glass and aluminium – now made it possible to build even higher and led to the design of simple buildings with clean lines, free of decorative patterns or ornamentation. This international style is much in evidence in Tokyo, the Défense area of Paris and Rio de Janeiro. New York has many such skyscrapers, including Lever House (1952) on Park Avenue and the Seagram Building (1958).

THE POST-MODERN PLAY ON SHAPE

The last thirty years have seen a reaction against the cold, dry international style and a return to a more fanciful architectural form that makes much play of unusual shapes, a style known as post-modern. From the skyscrapers of Times Square to those of Battery Park and the Sony Building (formerly the AT&T Building), architects such as Ieho Ming Pei, Philip Johnson and Cesare Pelli have built spectacular towers in which decorative elements, a return to classic

RENEWAL AND GENTRIFICATION

With urban renewal, the depopulation of the heart of New York has become a thing of the past. Developers are constantly moving into insalubrious and dilapidated districts and renovating them, and the well-to-do are now moving back to the city centre in a process of yuppy-led gentrification. Manhattan is endlessly being rebuilt, with the new skyscrapers and renovated office blocks of Midtown and the lofts of SoHo and Greenwich Village replacing the slums and workshops. Even the natural backdrops of *West Side Story* have disappeared and been replaced by the buildings of the Lincoln Center.

materials and references to the past are freely juxtaposed, albeit with a certain penchant for garishness.

MELTING POT OR TIME BOMB?

New York has long had a very diverse population, with people of different race, religion and origin living side by side, and it's precisely this that gives it its unique character and makes it a melting pot of ethnic cultures, traditions and languages. There's simply nowhere quite like it.

Latin-American, 25% African American, 7% Asian and only 43% Caucasian, the latter, consisting largely of Anglo-Saxons and Eastern Europeans, is becoming fewer year by year.

IN WHICH ETHNIC NEIGHBOURHOOD DO YOU BELONG?

Russian immigrants traditionally occupy the Brighton Beach district of Brooklyn and the Chinese congregate in Chinatown, in Manhattan and in Queens. Bronx and Harlem. Today, the ethnic groupings are still prevalent.

MINORITIES OLD AND NEW

In 1945 nine out of every ten New Yorkers were white, with immigrants coming almost

THE JEWISH COMMUNITY

New York ranks above Jerusalem and Tel Aviv as the largest Jewish city in the world, so much so that the words *New Yorker* are often

The Polish refugees live in Greenpoint and the old district of Little Italy, which has long since been abandoned by the Italians and is gradually being eaten away by Chinatown, whose population has grown five-fold in thirty years. Hispanics, meanwhile, rival African Americans for the exclusively from Europe. In 1965, when immigration quotas were abolished, nearly three million Jamaican, Dominican, Mexican, Korean, Pakistani, Indian and Chinese immigrants arrived to settle in New York. Nowadays, the picture is quite different, with New Yorkers comprising 25%

synonymous with 'Jewish' throughout the United States – which means you'll see plenty of kosher food shops. In the 1950s, many Jews left the Lower East Side and the other traditionally Jewish neighbour-hoods of Manhattan and went to live in Brooklyn and on Long Island.

CONFRONTATIONS

The arrival of immigrants from very diverse cultures can sometimes lead to interesting or violent confrontations. Even with the passing of time, the New York communities tend to remain separate, and mixed marriages are still a rare event. The Puerto Ricans think the Mexicans can't speak Spanish properly, while

the latter get on very well with the Greeks and Chinese, who find them work. There can be tensions between African Americans and Asians, and although they all consider themselves to be New Yorkers, the ethnic communities cling to their individuality, and maintain their own culture.

FESTIVAL CALENDAR

Late January/early February
Chinese New Year Chinatown.

March
St Patrick's Day (17 March) The Irish mark their patron saint's day with a parade on 5th Avenue from St Patrick's Church to 86th Street. The day usually ends with a Guinness in one of the many Irish pubs.
Greek Independence Day Parade (Sun. after 25 March) on 5th Avenue, with dancing and a procession in national costume.

April
Easter Parade on 5th Avenue.

May
Israeli Day Parade on 5th Avenue.

June
Puerto Rican Day Parade (2nd Sun. in the month) on 5th Avenue.

August
Harlem Weeks – a cultural ethnic festival with art, music, dance, fashion, cinema and sport.
St Stephen's Day Parade (middle of the month) mounted parade by the Hungarian community on E 86th Street.

September
Feast of San Gennaro – ten days of festivities in honour of the patron saint of Naples in Little Italy (Mulberry Street).

October
Pulaski Day Parade (beginning of the month) Polish festival on 5th Avenue.
Hispanic Day Parade (middle of the month) on 5th Avenue, between 57th and 86th Street.

November
Thanksgiving Day Parade (4th Thu. in the month) From 77th Street to Broadway.

December
Hannukah Week-long Jewish festival. One of the seven candles of the menorah (candelabrum) is lit each day.

NEW YORK, ART CAPITAL OF THE WORLD

Everyone will tell you that at the start of the new millennium New York is still firmly entrenched as the cultural centre of the Western world. Art is no longer just something to do or buy here – it has truly become a way of life.

GALLERIES AND MUSEUMS, THE ESSENTIAL SHOWCASES OF ART

With more than a hundred and fifty museums, four hundred art galleries, some remarkable libraries, and outstanding concert halls and theatres in Manhattan alone, New York is undeniably the cultural capital of the United States. Widespread private patronage stimulates artistic creativity and helps create an atmosphere of almost palpable cultural tension in the city.

INTERIOR DESIGN: ART FURNITURE

New York is home to a large number of designers who make original one-off pieces of decorative work and furniture.

They belong to the Art Furniture movement and their work using craft techniques is a slap in the face for mass-produced furniture. The movement's artists hope to make people think about the dangers of the technological, standardised way of life. A wide range of examples of the American decorative arts and design of every kind can be seen at the Cooper Hewitt National Design Museum (see p. 40).

FASHION: MADE TO MEASURE & DISPOSABLE

As undisputed centre of the American clothing industry, New York has long been a showcase of style and fashion. The young ready-to-wear designers display their collections in showrooms and if you want to keep abreast of all the latest trends that will be hitting the

American fashion headlines, you could try Charivari 57 (18 W 57th Street, between 5th and 6th Ave., ☎ 333 40 40), for example – it's a hothouse of young designers.

NEW MUSIC: EXPERIMENTS IN SOUND

New Music owes a great deal to the innovative work of the composers Charles Ives and John Cage. Extending the possibilities of percussion instruments, it seeks to incorporate jazz and, above all, rock. New Music is the music of Greenwich Village – of the lofts, experimental spaces and multimedia. Musicians such as Philip Glass and Laurie Anderson are good representatives of the genre. Log on to the SoundArt Foundation's website (www.soundart.org) to find out up-to-date information on concerts of all forms of contemporary music. *The* place for cutting-edge jazz is Knitting Factory (see p. 59).

THE PRESS

The major serious magazines, and in particular the *New York Review of Books* and *Commentary* (the former democratic and the latter conservative), are published in

New York. The most prestigious newspaper in the United States, the *New York Times*, also has its head office here. There are sixteen foreign-language dailies, up to a hundred ethnic weeklies and countless reviews in just about every language in the world. Don't miss the local neighbourhood publications such as *The Village Voice* – this paper in particular is a well respected free weekly. As well as some excellent writing and non-mainstream debate, it features up-to-the-minute listings.

ANDY WARHOL, POP ART'S STAR

In the early 1960s, Andy Warhol earned his living by drawing shoes for publicity campaigns and decorating shop windows. Then, at a time when America was in the throes of the Vietnam War and still reeling from the deaths of Martin Luther King, John F. Kennedy and Marilyn Monroe, he took to reproducing images of soup tins, Coca-Cola bottles and series of portraits of famous modern-day icons, such as Liz Taylor and Marlon Brando, using the technique of silk-screen printing. He launched the much-discussed pop art movement and his famous workshop, known as The Factory, became the meeting-place of all the smart, trendy inhabitants of Manhattan, including the members of the Velvet Underground rock band.

Marilyn Monroe, as seen by Andy Warhol.

THE CAPITAL OF THE 'PROMISED LAND'

New York owes the scale of its development to an outstanding geographical setting. Built on an island with one of the largest natural harbours in the world, the metropolis fascinated and attracted crowds of immigrants, who came here to seek their fortune.

Manhattan Island, late 19th-century engraving.

THE DISCOVERY OF THE SITE

Manhattan Island was discovered by the Florentine Verrazano in 1524, and in 1609 the Englishman Hudson, in the service of the Dutch, sailed up the river that bears his name. The site of New Amsterdam – the southern-most tip of Manhattan – was later chosen by the Dutch for strategic reasons. Captured by the English in 1664, the city was renamed New York in honour of the Duke of York, the future King James II. A century later, it became the first capital of the United States of America, a status it retained for five years, from 1785 to 1790.

CROSSROADS OF THE AMERICAN CONTINENT

New York took off in the 19th century thanks to its relative proximity to the Great Lakes (Fulton tested his steamer on the Hudson River in 1807) and the city quickly established

itself as the gateway to America. As the immigrants' port of disembarkation, it was here that the great railways, which allowed access to a vast back country stretching as far as the Rockies, converged from 1850 onwards. From 1860 to the end of the 19th century, New York grew in every way, with the population increasing rapidly. In the 20th century, the subway, the city transport system and the airports added the finishing touches to the great New York crossroads.

ELLIS ISLAND: GATEWAY TO THE PROMISED LAND

Ellis Island in the bay of New York is the place where were sometimes separated, it's here that immigrants were marked with chalk and given a new identity before being thrown into the New World.

the 17 million immigrants in transit to the rest of the United States disembarked between 1892 and 1954. Known as the 'Island of Tears' because families

Over time, the wooden huts where all new arrivals were processed were replaced by an Art Nouveau-style building. Now renovated and turned into a museum (see p. 35), it remains a moving testimony to all those who have passed through it.

LIBERTY LIGHTING THE WORLD

Off the southern tip of Manhattan stands New York's most famous monument, the Statue of Liberty. Sculpted by Auguste Bartholdi on a framework by Gustave Eiffel, the colossal statue was presented to the United States by France in 1886 and was restored by French and American craftsmen in 1986. The 46m/150ft high figure of Liberty holds the torch of freedom aloft in one hand, while in the other is a tablet dated 4 July 1776, the date of the American Declaration of Independence. Personifying liberty, it was used as a symbol by the Chinese demonstrators in Tiananmen Square in May 1989.

> 'Your torch lights up New York, but your light shines In every corner of the world.'
> *Melech Ravitch, 1883.*

THE LOWER EAST SIDE, CRADLE OF IMMIGRATION

The first district of New York to be settled by immigrants was the Lower East Side. Irish immigrants and later Jews from Central Europe made their homes here in dilapidated buildings without any proper sanitation. These miserable living conditions gave rise to a feeling of solidarity and the Lower East Side was the scene of growing social awareness. This in turn led to community organisation that has lasted to the present day. Despite its sometimes unwelcoming appearance, this district of Manhattan has become very fashionable and has several bars and trendy restaurants as well as shops belonging to the hottest designers.

THE STYLE JUNGLE

New York fashion can best be described as eclectic. Diversity and change are the watchwords, and everyone here dresses differently, with their own personal look – which is perhaps the essence of New York style. A few pointers will help you find your way around.

THE TECHNO AGE

It's now over ten years since the hypnotic electronic rhythms of techno first assaulted the eardrums of New York night-owls. The music has now spread far and wide thanks to the work of DJs, some of whom are the star attractions at the best social events. It's a world of machines with its own correspondingly futuristic looks involving a mixture of metallic-effect materials, with motifs and holograms liberally sewn on T-shirts.

If you want a personal taste of the experience, spend at least one evening in a trendy club such as *Tunnel* (see Nightlife section p. 118 for further information).

STYLE TO THE RHYTHMS OF RAP AND HIP-HOP

The importance of street trends should not be overlooked. In music, they're characterised by rap and hip-hop in general. A number of

movements have succeeded one another, from Old School to militant rap and gangster rap, but all with the same frenetic energy. Baggy trousers and the latest sneakers are

MAD ABOUT ACCESSORIES

New Yorkers are very keen on accessories, which add the finishing touch to any look. Shoe shops, for example,

the order of the day and among the favourite shops of these streetwear fans are Polo Ralph Lauren and Tommy Hilfiger.

JAMAICAN ROOTS

Reggae is still as popular as ever in New York. However, this mixture of work songs, spirituals and electric sounds, which originated in Jamaica and became popular the world over thanks to Bob Marley, isn't just a form of music, it's also an expression of a way of thinking and living.

Rastas are vegetarians, they don't drink alcohol, though they *do* smoke Ganja. Rather than cutting their hair, they allow it to grow into long, thick dreadlocks, and wear the distinctive red, yellow and green colours of the Ethiopian flag.

HARDCORE PUNK

Hardcore punk first swept New York over twenty years ago, but it still hasn't lost its vitality and fans often gather around St Mark's Place. For a ridiculously small sum of money, you can have a made-to-measure haircut (i.e. have your head shaved) in Astor Place Hair Designers.

URBAN STREETWEAR

Streetwear is back on the map again with a functional, cargo-influenced look that is a mix of military and workwear. It's all 'utility chic' or 'American street', with lots of patriotic Stars and Stripes accessories. Urban streetwear hipsters

display mile upon mile of stiletto heels, platform shoes and trainers, while jewellery and leather shops offer a wide range of goods (bags, belts, gloves, etc.), from timeless classics that will never go out of fashion to the latest trends and the most avant-garde designs. Careful attention to detail and personalisation are often taken to extremes with tattooing and highly unusual body piercing.

still love their jeans though, and 'hoodies' are all the rage. Try out the multimedia centres where you can sip tea as you surf the Internet while watching a performance on a video screen and listening with one ear to the latest music. Whatever your personal choice of style, with the diverse range of fashion you'll see on the streets of New York, you're bound to fit in.

THE SOUNDS OF THE CITY

New York has a buzzing music scene, and the creativity is backed up by a prosperous and highly competitive record industry. From the classics to collectors items, the prices are unbeatable. Make the most of the opportunity to top up your CD collection.

MUSIC PARADISE

Record chain stores, such as Tower Records, are now widespread in New York. They offer not only a very wide choice but also low prices, sometimes with the added attraction of special offers. However, chain stores often mean a supermarket atmosphere. If it's something more interesting you're looking for, small record stores are the places to go. They sometimes have collector's items and secondhand discs and vinyl records. You can make amazing finds and pick up incredible bargains as you sift through their highly specialised selections. The atmosphere is certainly much warmer and you can ask the record dealers for advice, as well as listening to the recordings of your choice.

MUSIC AT COST PRICE

Old-style vinyl records and CDs are much cheaper here than elsewhere – roughly two thirds or even half the price. The reason for this is quite simple – Americans don't pay VAT and their recording industry is very highly developed.

However, price isn't the only advantage – some records have original American covers rarely found outside the US.

VINYL MAKES A COMEBACK

Contrary to the current vogue for CDs, vinyl records are in no danger of disappearing. In fact, they're currently growing in popularity, especially since DJs have brought them back into fashion. From rap to techno, the music of today has given vinyl pressings back their usefulness and charm. They're essential for mixes, scratches and other sound effects. Some special editions are made of coloured or special plastic, but the sound is not as good as the traditional black vinyl.

BRAND NAMES AT BARGAIN PRICES

Hi-fi equipment is cheap in New York, where you'll find every conceivable make and model. With all the latest record decks, CD systems, DVD players, mixer boards, special effects pedals and headphones on offer, it's impossible not to find what you need. There's even a district devoted to musical instruments, so if you're looking for a much-coveted 1968 Fender Stratocaster or the saxophone of your dreams, take a look in the shop windows on 48th Street (between 6th and 7th Ave., see p. 106-7). But remember to watch out for voltage, plugs, compatability and customs duty (see p. 81).

THE SPECIALISED PRESS: FANZINES & SOUND REVIEWS

Often specialising in a particular type of music (jazz, reggae, techno, etc.), the music press publishes the calendar of concerts and other musical events taking place in the Big Apple (or you could check out the listings at www.ny.com/nightlife). Even if you're not a particular fan of the music, it's worth taking a look at these magazines for the illustrations alone. Some, such as *Mad Planet,* which specialises in ska, are illustrated by highly imaginative graphic artists. You can find them in specialist record shops.

PIRATE TAPES AND HOME-MADE MUSIC

As you walk through New York, you'll often come across street vendors selling cassettes recorded and mixed by DJs themselves at home. These make entertaining listening, are inexpensive and can be a very good way of discovering the latest newcomers to the music scene. Flea markets can also be a useful place to pick up musical bargains – they often have huge displays of cassette recordings on sale for under $8.

SPORTSWEAR AND WORKOUTS

Sportswear, having made the transition from the stadium and track to the street, retains its popularity and looks like it's here to stay. Comfortable, tough and easy-care, its individual elements can be mixed and matched, allowing everyone to create their own look. For manufacturers trying to get their brands known it's a booming market.

SNEAKERS: AN INDISPENSABLE ACCESSORY

Sneakers are an integral

part of the streetwear look and a number of New York shops specialise in them. They're actually so fashionable that it's by no means rare to see people wearing them with city suits or skirts. NikeTown (see p. 93) or Reebok have very extensive selections and you can be sure of finding all the very latest styles. Otherwise, stroll down Broadway, between 8th and Broome Street, where you'll find lots of stores selling trainers (sneakers). The prices should be the same, but do shop around.

SPORTS GOODS

A whole culture has grown up in the US in response to the desire for youthful, healthy bodies. You can see people playing pelota in East Harlem, practising Tai Chi in Central Park, playing basketball in the street and jogging just about everywhere. Sports shops often resemble huge hypermarkets and are worth a visit. At Paragon Sports (see p. 93), for example, you'll find items that are both practical and fashionable, such as roller-blades, but you'll also come across the most unlikely gadgets, such as a pushchair you can attach to your belt when you go jogging with your baby (who of course wears a helmet), or a watch that monitors your heartbeat and tells you the number of calories you've burned, as well as giving you the time in Tokyo.

THE NAME OF THE GAME

Some people prefer discreet labels and logos, while others are perfectly happy to wear the brands of their clothes emblazoned in large letters and treat their manufacturers to a little free advertising in the process. Branded goods are more expensive but often better quality, so that could be just the excuse you need to stock up on Nike, Reebok and Champion T-shirts and sweatshirts. They'll last far longer and probably cost less than at home, and you'll have the pleasure of parading around in designs you can't buy elsewhere. You may also find counterfeit goods, but if you buy these you should be aware that you're encouraging an illegal trade.

diets are, of course, careful to eat plenty of protein, and the more beauty conscious use the latest scientifically developed skincare products to help them prepare and maintain their tans, with or without the sun.

DENIM FROM NÎMES OR JEANS FROM GENOA

From the Western jeans of yesteryear to classic 501s or up-to-the-minute baggies (extra-wide 560s), blue denim has become the global emblem of leisurewear. In San Francisco in 1850, Levi Strauss had the brilliant idea of making trousers out of a fabric from the Italian port of Genoa (which was eventually distorted into 'jeans'). From the world of work to the world of high fashion, by way of leisurewear, jeans have gradually found popularity with young and old alike. Three major brands, Levi Strauss, Lee and Wrangler, have been responsible for establishing the reputation of this rough but tough fabric. If you want to find authentic 501s for under $20, make a beeline for Unique Clothing on Broadway, where you can be sure of finding a bargain.

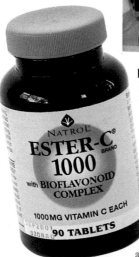

PRODUCTS FOR THE SPORTY

New Yorkers are very keen on keeping fit – mineral water, salad and some fruit will suffice for lunch and they often take cocktails of vitamins with their meals. Whole chains of outlets, such as Vitamin Shop or GNC, are devoted to them. Body builders and those on low calorie

SHOW BUSINESS

Performances of every kind play a significant part in the daily lives of New Yorkers, especially as many of them are free. In summer, Central Park is filled with the sound of operatic arias and techno music, while budding dancers and actors set up makeshift stages and perform on street corners. Not content just to be a spectacle in itself, New York can also claim to be the performance capital of the world.

ON AND OFF BROADWAY

The latest shows can be seen in Times Square, where the famous Broadway musicals and theatrical events are staged. But New York theatre isn't just restricted to this celebrated avenue. You can also see performances at the Lyceum, the oldest theatre in New York, or venture into the realm of Off-Off Broadway with alternative productions by the Actors & Directors Lab or Black Theater Alliance, who regularly stage interesting and innovative works by contemporary playwrights.

THE RHYTHM OF THE DANCE

New York acquired its status as dance capital shortly after the end of the war. At that time, Martha Graham was forging the way ahead towards modern dance. With the arrival of Merce Cunningham on the scene in the 1950s, American

choreography was enriched with a whole new aesthetic as his avant-garde experiments spread throughout the city. The 1960s were a time of new creativity and greater freedom, and present-day choreographers, such as Trisha Brown, have extended their activities to art galleries and lofts.

PERFORMANCE ART JOINS THE MAINSTREAM

Performance art (manifested in 'happenings') is neither theatre, cinema, dance nor music, but all of these at once. The performance artist works with sounds, rhythms and images, which he then proceeds to transform. Thanks to the new media and to more and more varied visual and sound recording techniques, the concept of performance art

has broadened. Today's happenings are no longer confined to art galleries but have found their way into clubs and theatres, especially those of Chelsea (see p.60-61).

LIGHTS, CAMERA, ACTION!

New York is 'cinegenic'. Since the golden age of the 1930s and 40s, until Woody Allen, Sydney Pollack and Francis F. Coppola appeared on the scene, all the big directors have fallen under its spell.

With seats in the region of $10, New Yorkers often go to the cinema. There are many cinemas, and previews are very popular. When New York movie fans want something a little different to the big productions, there are a number of places that are worth a visit: the MoMA (Museum of Modern Art), one of the temples of the avant-garde, the Angelika

DEPARTMENT STORES – SHOP TILL YOU DROP

The New York department stores are the image of the American dream. Many started out as small, ordinary shops serving a local clientele. From these humble beginnings, they later prospered and became symbols of elegance. They are often vast labyrinths, so if you want to explore all the various departments, make sure you leave plenty of time.

A SHOWCASE OF GOOD TASTE

Everyone agrees that if you want to get an idea of New York chic, both traditional and modern, you only need to take a walk round one of the city's department stores. The shop windows are fabulous, and the goods are remarkably well displayed on the stands inside for maximum temptation! Stores often ask prominent designers and stylists to create original lines of articles for them (ranging from clothes to household goods and linens). The outright winner of the award for elegance in this area is undoubtedly Saks Fifth Avenue.

UNBEATABLE QUALITY AND VARIETY

From attaché cases and dinner services to sunglasses and interior decoration, you'll find everything imaginable in the New York department stores. They all have different specialities – Barneys has become a showcase for trendy fashion, while Bloomingdale's is reputed for its household goods and delicatessen. One thing all these establishments have in common is the quality of the goods on offer, which sometimes justifies their high prices.

FULL PRICE OR BARGAIN BASEMENT

Prices are a little higher than elsewhere but are still affordable when exchange rates are favourable. New Yorkers, for their part, wait for the sales, which offer real bargains in clothing, household goods and interior decoration. The atmosphere is electric and it's a good idea to have a look round in advance to be sure of finding the article you want. However, sale goods aren't always exchangeable or refunded (ask when you pay). Sales take place at the start of the year, as

was the former captain of a whaling vessel who changed tack and went into business. The store has a famous beauty products department, where you can get a free facial and make-up plus free samples. It also organises the annual 4th July

down Broadway every year between 9am and noon on the 4th Thursday in November. The 22nd November 2002 marks the 75th anniversary of the event.

well as between late June and early July. Take our tip and be there when the stores open.

MACY'S, THE BIGGEST STORE IN THE WORLD

The biggest shop in the United States could well also be the biggest in the world. It takes up a whole block all by itself. The red star that is the shop's logo is a reminder of the founder's tattoo. R. H. Macy

(Independence Day) firework display and the Thanksgiving Day parade that winds its way

ADDRESSES

Henri Bendel
712 5th Avenue
☎ 247 11 00 (see p. 83).

Bergdorf Goodman
754 5th Avenue (at 57th Street)
☎ 753 73 00
Open Mon.-Fri. 10am-7pm
(Thu. to 8pm), Sat. noon-6pm.

Bloomingdale's
1000 3rd Avenue (at 59th Street)
☎ 705 20 00
Open Mon.-Wed. 10am-8.30pm
(Thu.-Fri. to 10pm, Sat. to 7pm),
Sun. 11am-7pm (see p. 83).

Lord & Taylor
424 5th Avenue (at 38th Street)
☎ 391 33 44
Open Mon., Tue., Sat. 10am-7pm (Thu. & Fri. to 8.30pm),
Wed. 9am-8.30pm, Sun.
11am-7pm.

Macy's
151 W 34th Street
☎ 494 46 62
Open Mon.-Sat. 10am-8.30pm,
Sun. 11am-7pm (see p. 37).

Saks Fifth Avenue
611 5th Avenue (at 50th Street)
☎ 753 40 00
Open Mon.-Wed., Fri.-Sun.
10am-6.30pm, Thu. 10am-8pm.

Barneys
660 Madison Avenue (at 61st St.)
☎ 826 89 00
Open Mon.-Fri. 10am-8pm,
(Sat. to 7pm), Sun. noon-6pm
(see p. 88).

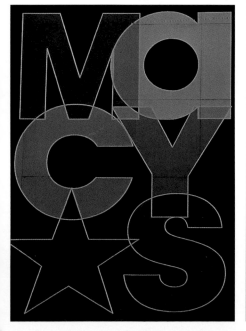

A SHOPPING PARADISE

New York is the global epicentre of consumerism and it's virtually impossible to come away empty-handed. Here are a few original shopping ideas which are excellent value for money and have the added bonus of being difficult to find elsewhere.

PHARMACEUTICAL FANTASIES

Originally prescribed as a cure for jet lag, the wonder drug melatonin is now parading as an anti-ageing pill. Your trendy friends will probably ask you to bring some back with you. It's just one example among many of the vast range of pharmaceutical products available over the counter. Cosmetics are often cheaper than you may be used to, including the famous Estée Lauder and Revlon skincare products (you'll find them on sale at Duane Reade, a large drugstore chain). And if you'd like a genuine New York look for an evening, why not pop into a beauty parlour for false nails and false eyelashes in the most amazing shapes and colours.

NATURE'S WAY

For some time now, New Yorkers have fantasised about a return to nature. Health foods, both vegetarian and macrobiotic, have their faithful fans, and so-called health stores are springing up in ever-increasing numbers. These not only sell food, but a range of beauty products, perfumes, household accessories and stationery, all 100% natural or recycled. Take the opportunity to buy presents for your 'green' friends – there's a very wide choice and the prices offer really great value.

HOUSEHOLD LINEN

Used on its own or in a mixture with another fibre, American cotton is renowned. It doesn't shrink in the wash and it keeps its shape perfectly. Whether it's bath towels, bath-robes,

COMIC BOOKS AND COLLECTORS' ITEMS

Created by such notables as Stan Lee and Jack Kerby, American comics relating the adventures of such superheroes as Batman and Spiderman are the foremost collectors' items in the United States. Originally designed for children, comic books quickly became popular with a wider readership and new heroes with more human faces appeared on the scene. New York offers some excellent shops where you can uncover real gems of this typically American artwork, but expect to pay top prices for them.

merchandising and their shops are often well stocked. You'll easily find a wide variety of posters, calendars and writing paper as well as tableware, linen, jewellery, T-shirts and household objects that are sure to please. Some shops even have a despatch service, which allows you to be a little less weighed down on the way home.

GADGETS GALORE

New York is an endless source of gadgets, both useful (check out the computerised toaster with voice synthesiser!), useless, whacky or simply decorative. Electronics often play an important part in the

sheets, duvet covers or table linen you're looking for, you'll find some outstanding bargains, especially in the department stores. Just remember you may need to pay more to get the very best quality

REPRODUCTIONS AND ART BOOKS

Many New York bookshops specialise in art books but also sell high-quality reduced and secondhand books. The city museums, which also publish very fine art catalogues and books, cash in to the full on

more sophisticated and spectacular of them. If you simply can't live without a personal cooling system (a sort of portable air-conditioning unit that you wear around your neck) or a phone in the shape of a Harley Davidson or a basketball, you'll have hours of fun exploring the specialist shops.

New York Practicalities

New York may be intimidating in size, but its very simple street plan and efficient public transport system make it easy to find your way and move about in the city.

MAP READING

From south to north, Manhattan Island is made up of three distinct parts: **Downtown**, the city centre, lies in the southernmost part of the island and stretches as far as 14th Street; **Midtown**, as its name suggests, occupies the middle of Manhattan and stretches from 14th Street to the region of 59th Street. Finally, **Uptown** consists of the whole northern part of the island above 59th Street.

New York was built on a grid plan, with straight streets and avenues crossing one another and numbered in a very simple way. This geometrical layout enables you to find your way easily. To put it quite simply, the streets are designated by numbers that increase as you move from Downtown to Uptown (1st, 2nd, 3rd Street, etc.). The avenues, on the other hand, are numbered from east to west; with the exception of the first four, which are located Downtown and are designated by the letters of the alphabet (Avenues A, B, C and D).

A few of the avenues actually have names and these act as landmarks in a world of numbers. The best-known of these are probably Broadway and Madison Avenue. At the level of the West Village, the streets also have proper names instead of numbers. In the Financial District, which forms the historic heart of the city and lies on the southernmost tip of the island, the grid plan gives way to a more anarchic jumble of streets.

GETTING ABOUT

BY SUBWAY

The subway is a very practical way of getting about the city and runs 24 hours a day. Operated by NYC Transit, there are 468 stations with lines designated by numbers or letters, though some lines are known by unofficial names, such as the Broadway Line for 1, 2, 3 or the Lexington Line for 4, 5 or 6. You can avoid stopping at every station by taking express trains, which only stop at stations marked with a large dot on plans. The stations at which express trains stop can be recognised by the sign on the front. Trains travelling north have a sign saying Uptown and those travelling south have one saying Downtown.

MetroCards allow an unlimited number of journeys by subway and bus. Each journey costs $1.50, but if you buy a $15 card, you get 11 rides for the price of 10. When you swipe the card, the fare is valid for up to 2 hours and will cover certain transfers, but without the card you have to pay again each time you transfer. For those wishing to move around a great deal an Unlimited Ride Card is recommended, costing $17 for 7 days and $63 for 30 or you can get a Fun Pass for $4 which allows unlimited rides in a day. MetroCards can be bought at subway stations with cash, credit or debit cards.

BY BUS

Buses are a very good way to discover New York as long as you're not in too much of a hurry. They're slow because they often get stuck in traffic, especially at the end of the day – gridlock is a common feature of life in New York. However, if you don't buy a weekly MetroCard, they're a less expensive way to travel than the subway since you can buy a transfer ticket (from the driver of the first bus you get on) and change buses without having to buy another ticket. You can use subway tokens or a MetroCard, or buy a ticket on the bus, but make sure you have the right money – bus drivers flatly refuse to give change.

A useful number for information about the subway and buses in several languages is: ☎ (718) 330 48 47.

The subway, like the buses, runs 24 hours a day. It's quick and convenient but unfortunately not the safest place to be late at night, so you may prefer to take a taxi back to your hotel.

BY TAXI

New York wouldn't be New York without the countless battered yellow cabs that race through the streets at top speed, paying no attention to the potholes. The drivers rarely speak good English so make sure you give them clear directions. Try to tell them the cross road corresponding to the section of the street you want to get to, eg. 350 E 39th Street at 5th Avenue. If you don't, you may find yourself driving around for some time with the meter ticking. Fortunately, taxi rides aren't expensive – don't forget to give the driver a tip, though – roughly 20% of the fare, or more if you have any luggage. A word of advice: be prepared for a wait in the rush hour – you'll find everyone is trying to get a taxi and they all have their own way of getting one before anyone else, so make sure your're quick off the mark.

ON FOOT

To really see New York and get the feel of it, you have to go about on

foot. You'll be amazed by the distance New Yorkers can cover every day in the city. It's far cheaper and of course you'll see much more of the city this way; the streets are full of life and there's a surprise waiting for you on every street corner. You have to walk the length of the big avenues to understand the New Yorkers' love of their city. Pedestrians are always careful to obey the highway code, so avoid crossing the road at random and always look for a pedestrian crossing, otherwise you might be in for a telling off by a cop or might even get knocked down.

BICYCLE HIRE

With so many reckless car and taxi drivers about, it isn't a good idea to ride a bike in the city streets. It's much better to keep push-bikes for quiet rides in Central Park or the Village.

Pedal Pushers

☎ 288 55 92
1306 2nd Avenue
(between 68th and
69th Streets).
Open every day except
Tue. 10am-6pm.
$10-60 a day.

Bike and Fitness

☎ 249 93 44
242 E 79th Street,
(near 2nd Avenue).
open every day 10am-7pm.
$10-50 a day.

TOGA Bike Shop

110 West End Avenue
(at 64th Street)
☎ 799 96 25
Open Mon.-Fri. 11am-7pm
(Thu. to 7.30pm), Sat. 10am-6pm, Sun. 11am-6pm.
$30 for 24 hours.

PHONES

Making a phone call in New York is neither difficult nor expensive provided you avoid ringing from your hotel room, where a tax will be added to the cost of all phone calls. If you're calling from a public phone, make sure you have plenty of change. You'll need at least $7 in quarters (a total of 28 coins!) for an international call. To call abroad you'll need the following prefixes:

To the UK:

☎ 011 44 + local area code, leaving out the first 0 of the UK number

To Ireland:

☎ 011 353 + local area code

To Australia:

☎ 011 61 + local area code

To New Zealand:

☎ 011 64 + local area code

It costs 25 cents to make a 3-minute local call from a public pay phone. If you think you're going to make frequent calls buy a phone card, which are available from most newsagents, delis and kiosks. They make it easy for you to make long-distance phone calls without having to load your pockets down with coins. American numbers consist of seven digits preceded by the area code. The most common codes in New York are: Manhattan, 212; and Brooklyn, the Bronx, Queens and Staten Island, 718.

If you want to call outside the area you're in, dial 1 followed by the area code of the number you're dialling.

All freephone numbers start with the prefix 800. If you want telephone information about New York, dial 411. For telephone information about any other state, dial 1, followed by the area code and then 555 1212.

THE POST OFFICE

The postal service between the USA and Europe is fairly fast. It usually takes about a week for letters to reach Europe from New York and a little longer the other way round. If you need to send something urgently, delivery services such as **Federal Express** will arrange to deliver the following day (☎ 1 800 463 33 39).

Stamps can be bought at post offices, which are usually open from 8.30am to 6pm Monday to Friday and on Saturday mornings. The General Post Office (421 8th Avenue at 33rd Street), stays open 24 hours a day. You can buy ordinary stamps there but also more unusual series, if you're a collector.

Mailboxes are large, blue and have *US Mail* written on them, but foreigners have often mistaken them for rubbish bins!

MUSEUM OPENING TIMES

Most museums are open from 9 or 10am to 5.30 or 6pm, but opening

times vary from place to place. Museums have late evenings once or twice a week and most are closed on Mondays and holidays. The Solomon R. Guggenheim Museum is closed on Thursdays and MoMa is closed on Wednesdays. It's best to check with the museum in question if you don't want to miss a particular exhibition.

CITYPASS

The Citypass gets you into seven famous New York attractions for just $38 ($31 for children aged 12-17), including the American Museum of Natural History, the Guggenheim Museum, the Intrepid Sea Air Space Museum, MoMA, the Empire State Building, the Circle Line Harbour Cruise and the Whitney Museum of Modern Art. Lasting 9 days, the pass can be purchased at any of the attractions or online at www.citypass.net.

The tip of Manhattan

The southern tip of Manhattan is where you are most conscious of being on an island and from where you can see the Statue of Liberty. The district is home to the city's financial centre and of course the former site of the World Trade Center.

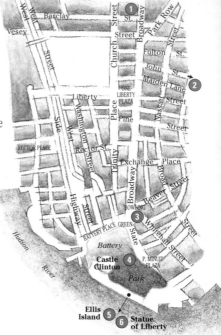

❶ Woolworth Building★★

233 Broadway (at Barclay Street, southern tip of City Hall Park).

Built in 1913 by the architect Cass Gilbert in a neo-Gothic style, this was, until 1930, the tallest skyscraper in the world. Just recently, it belonged to the famous Woolworth chain. It's particularly worth visiting for the elegant vaults of its entrance hall decorated with blue, green and gold mosaics. Take a look, too, at the exterior sculptures with

their superbly carved moulding – they're really quite exquisite.

❷ South Street Seaport★★

Water Street to the East River, between John Street and Peck Slip
☎ **732 76 78 (general information)**

South Street Seaport's unusual architecture has a certain undeniably provincial charm and allows you to get a feel for the maritime history of the city. Here you'll find a number of interesting things to see, including the lighthouse built to commemorate the Titanic at the corner of Water and Fulton Streets and the many restaurants and wine bars that line Fulton Street down to the

sea, not forgetting Pier 17 and its commercial centre. The view of Brooklyn Bridge is wonderful. The Seaport Museum at 12 Fulton Street (☎ 748 86 00) retraces the history of the city as a port through a collection of galleries, historic ships and 19th-century buildings.

➌ National Museum of the American Indian★★★
George Gustav Heye Center
US Custom House
1 Bowling Green
☎ 514 37 00
Open every day 10am-5pm
(Thu. to 8pm)
Entry free.

This museum devoted to American Indian culture occupies two floors of the former US Custom House. The displays are organised by theme, region and tribe and include both old objects and contemporary Amerindian works. The exhibitions are mounted entirely by native American Indians.

➍ Battery Park and Castle Clinton★★

This delightful garden bordering the southern tip of Manhattan takes its name from the battery of cannons on Castle Clinton. Today you can buy tickets for the tour of the Statue of Liberty and Ellis Island here, but it's mainly a pleasant place to relax. Take a walk alongside the Hudson river and breathe in some fresh sea air.

➎ Ellis Island★★★
Ferry leaves from Battery Park every day 9am-5.30pm.
☎ 269 57 55

Recently renovated, the 'Island of Tears' has become a place of pilgrimage for large numbers of Americans. More than 16 million people passed through here between 1892 and 1954. Moving graffiti left on the walls include portraits, dates and the outlines of boats. In the exhibition rooms, you can see a variety of artefacts, including old passports, logbooks, musical instruments

and souvenirs of passengers in transit. Do note that new security measures are in place and all passengers will be screened.

➏ The Statue of Liberty★★★
Ferry leaves from Battery Park every day 9am-5.30pm
15min. crossing
☎ 269 57 55.

This giant neo-Classical statue was built in 1884 by the French sculptor Frédéric-Auguste Bartholdi, though Gustave Eiffel, of Tower fame, also made his mark on it by building the iron scaffolding. You can climb right to the top of the statue and visit the crown but you'll need a little patience as the queues are very long. Security has recently been tightened, so allow extra time and bring photo ID with you. Don't miss the museum in the pedestal of the statue, which traces the history of its construction. The best view of all, however, is the one from the boat – you can see the whole Bay of Manhattan stretching before you, with the Statue of Liberty in the foreground.

11/09/01, THE DAY THAT CHANGED THE WORLD

No one is ever likely to forget the attack on the World Trade Center on Tuesday 11th September 2001 (or 9/11 as the Americans call it), in which 2,823 people lost their lives. The complex was made up of seven buildings, of which the Twin Towers were the most famous and most symbolic, both to Americans and the wider world. Huge damage was caused, and at the time of going to press, the site, known as 'Ground Zero', is 60-ft (1,968-m) hole, with its future yet to be determined. The World Trade Center Viewing Platform, located at Broadway and Fulton Street, is open every day 9am-8pm (☎ 732 76 78). Free tickets are available from the South Street Seaport Museum's ticket booth at Fulton and South Street on Pier 16. The booth is open 10am-6pm or until no further tickets are available. Two tickets per person are distributed on a first-come, first-served basis.

From the Empire State Building to Times Square

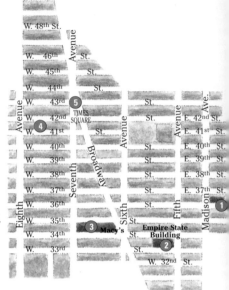

The Empire State Building is the most legendary skyscraper in the world and Times Square is one of the most magical spots in New York. Make your way from the great heights to the bright lights.

and Middle Ages. The museum is also home to a number of interesting and valuable documents. In the East Room, for example, whose walls are covered with frescoes depicting the signs of the zodiac and historical characters, you can see the illuminated manuscript of the *Apocalypse*, together with one of the twenty-two original copies of the American Declaration of Independence of 1776.

❶ Morgan Library ★★
29 E 36th Street
☎ 685 06 10
www.morganlibrary.org
Open Tue.-Thu. 10.30am-5pm, Fri. 10.30am-8pm,
Sat. 10.30am-6pm,
Sun. noon-6pm.

This Italian Renaissance-style palace was built for J. Pierpont Morgan in 1902 to house his collection of rare books, several thousand of which date from the Renaissance

❷ Empire State Building ★★★
350 5th Avenue (at 34th St.)
☎ 736 31 00
Open Mon.-Fri. 10am-midnight, Sat.
& Sun. 9.30am-midnight
(last lift 11.30pm)
Entry charge.

The Empire State Building may no longer be the tallest skyscraper in the world, but

it's still the most famous and a major New York landmark. The 102-storey building took two years to build at the start of the 1930s crisis and stands 450m/1,454ft high. The best time to visit it is on a fine evening, when the sun is just setting in the mists of New Jersey and the lights of New

York are sparkling far below. The longest queue is on the second level (the 86th floor), where you have to wait for a lift to take you to the renowned 102nd floor. Try to be patient – the view from the top is well worth the wait.

❸ Macy's ★
Herald Square
151 W 34th Street
(between Broadway and 7th Ave.)
☎ 695 44 00
Open Mon.-Sat. 10am-8.30pm, Sun. 11am-7pm (stays open later over the Christmas period).

❺ TIMES SQUARE ★★★
Broadway (at 7th Ave.)
☎ 768 15 60 (Times Square Visitor Center)

It would be a crime to come to New York without visiting Times Square, particularly at night. Voted the best place to celebrate New Year's Eve in 2001, it plays host to all the big musicals and famous Broadway shows. It's all lights, billboards, crowds and sheer energy – a 24-hour circus and the public face of New York. Watch NBC and ABC on a giant screen or MTV at the corner of 45th Street. Don't miss it.

'The world's largest store! If you haven't seen Macy's, you haven't seen New York.' – at least according to Macy's advertising slogan. The gigantic department store, which occupies a whole block, can be recognised by its famous star. It may have lost some of its former prestige but you really can find everything you need here, including an animal grooming department. Several floors are devoted to fashion and designer wear, while the whole of the ground floor is taken up by cosmetics and perfumes. The sales are a time of mass hysteria.

❹ Madame Tussaud's New York ★★★
234 W 42nd Street
(between 7th and 8th Ave.)
☎ 1 800 246 88 72
Open Thu.-Fri. 10am-6pm, Fri.-Sat. 10am-10pm
www.madame-tussauds.com

The famous Wax Museum from London opened its doors in New York at the end of 2000. It has various themes, and the one not to miss is the 'Opening Night Party' with all the A-list American celebrities enjoying an elaborate Italian baroque garden party in full swing. Some of the portraits are so lifelike it's scary. Samuel L Jackson, Morgan Freeman, Elton John and Woody Allen are particularly impressive. The French Revolution area is pretty realistic, so watch out if you have little ones with you.

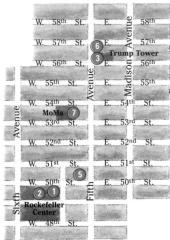

Around MoMA and the Rockefeller Center

MoMA is the intellectual heart of this lively district. Around it lies a paradise for shoppers, with the vast Rockefeller Center, like a town within a town itself, and the prestigious shops of 5th Avenue, including Tiffany's.

❶ The Rockefeller Center★★

W 48th-51st Street (between 5th & 6th Ave.)
☎ 632 39 75

The brainchild of John D Rockefeller during the Depression of the 1930s, today the Rockefeller Center is a vast complex of offices, shops, theatres and cinemas. The 250,000 people who work here mingle daily with local residents, 5th Avenue shoppers and those who simply come to see the wonderful golden statue of Prometheus surrounded by the flags of the United Nations member countries. In winter, try your hand at ice-skating or admire the huge Christmas tree. One of the most interesting places in the complex is the International Building, located behind the statue of Atlas.

❷ The Rainbow Room ★★

30 Rockefeller Center (65th floor)
☎ 632 51 00
Open every day noon-3pm, 5.30pm-midnight.

For a table with an amazing view, try the Rainbow Grill

on the 65th floor. There's a restaurant and piano bar, with live jazz played between 8pm and midnight. The cuisine is Italian, but you can just come for a drink. Nearby is the main ballroom where you can enjoy an evening of dinner and dancing in a 'Fred and Ginger' atmosphere accompanied by a big band. There's a fixed price menu (either $110 or $140) and the dress code is smart (open every day 7pm-1am).

❸ Trump Tower ★

725 5th Avenue (at 56th St.)
Open to the public 5-10pm.

Ex-golden boy Donald Trump gave his name to this 58-storey pink marble tower, which he had built by the architect Der

Scutt in 1983. The apartments are rented by celebrities, such as Michael Jackson and Steven Spielberg, when passing through. Five floors are entirely devoted to some of the world's most exclusive shops and there's a marvellous view of 5th Avenue from the fifth floor of the shopping centre.

❹ Hammacher Schlemmer ★★
147 East 57th Street
(between 3rd and Lexington Ave.)
☎ 421 90 00
Open Mon.-Sat. 10am-6pm.

Anyone who thinks they've seen it all should take a look round this large, six-storey shop. Here in a high-tech setting, the most unlikely gadgets are lying in wait for them, from electronic cat flaps to pith helmets with solar-powered fans. They may not exactly be practical but they're decorative and great fun!

❺ St Patrick's Cathedral ★★
5th Avenue
(between E 50th & 51st St.)
☎ 753 22 61
Open Sun.-Fri. 6.45am-9.45pm, Sat. 8am-8.45pm.

This is New York's most famous church and America's largest Roman Catholic cathedral. Its neo-Gothic architecture (1879) is

reminiscent of that of many European cathedrals. The stained glass windows were mostly built by craftsmen from Chartres and Nantes, and the controversial Cardinal O'Connor was buried here in 2000.

❻ Tiffany & Co. ★★
727 5th Avenue (at 57th St.)
☎ 755 80 00
Open Mon.-Fri. 10am-7pm, Sat. 10am-6pm.

It all began at the start of the century, when Louis Comfort Tiffany designed his famous lamps which you can see at the New York Historical Society (see p. 51) and sensational

❼ MUSEUM OF MODERN ART ★★★
☎ 708 94 00
NB: Due to a huge rebuilding project, MoMA will move in July 2002 from its home in 53rd Street to Queens. The Manhattan building is due to be completed in early 2005. Its temporary address is:
42-20 33rd Street (at Queens Boulevard)
Subway 33rd St. (line 7)
Open Sat.-Tue. & Thu. 10.30am-5.45pm, Fri. 10.30am-8.15pm
Entry charge ('pay as you wish' Fri. after 4.30pm).

The Museum of Modern Art, known simply as 'MoMA', houses a very fine collection of 20th-century works, all beautifully arranged. It's ideal for people who just like to wander around, discovering the gems for themselves. One room is reserved for Monet's Water Lilies, while Picasso, Miró, Matisse and all the other great artists are also well represented. Don't miss the Demoiselles d'Avignon, a major work painted by Picasso in Paris in 1907. There's also an area dedicated to photography, which stages fascinating temporary exhibitions. While you're in Queens, visit the P.S.1 Museum, another excellent contemporary art centre, 22-25 Jackson Avenue (at 46th Ave.), ☎ 1 718 784 20 84, www.ps1.org.

Art Nouveau jewellery. Since then, Tiffany's has become something of an institution. Nowadays Paloma Picasso designs the most spectacular pieces at equally spectacular prices. You'll need a credit card if you want to buy anything but window shopping is free.

Around the Metropolitan Museum of Art

Some of the buildings may look a touch cold and forbidding, but this ultra-chic district will be just what art lovers are looking for. Row upon row of museums stretch the length of 5th Avenue (the 'Museum Mile'), surrounded by many shops that are worth a visit.

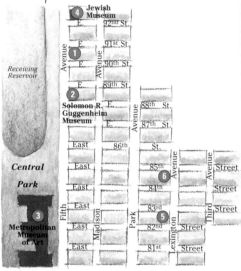

❶ Cooper Hewitt National Design Museum ★★

2 E 91st Street (at 5th Ave.)
☎ 849 84 00
Open Tue. 10am-9pm, Wed.-Sat. 10am-5pm, Sun. noon-5pm.
Entry charge, free Tue. 5-9pm.

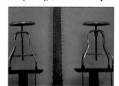

The museum is housed in a mansion which once belonged to Andrew Carnegie, one of the richest men in the world. Recently renovated, the oak-panelled hallway still retains its original decoration. Here you can see displays of the decorative arts and design, featuring furniture, porcelain and fabrics.

❷ Solomon R. Guggenheim Museum ★★★

1071 5th Avenue
(at 89th St.)
☎ 423 35 00
Open Mon.-Wed. and Sun. 9am-6pm, Fri.-Sat. 9am-8pm
Entry charge.

The building itself is a splendid example of contemporary architecture. Designed and built in large part by Frank Lloyd Wright in 1959, the spiral-shaped Guggenheim is a temple of art – from the Impressionists (Degas, Manet, Van Gogh and the rest) to the minimalists and conceptualists of the 1960s, most movements are represented here, including Expressionism, Cubism, Abstractionism and Surrealism. An absolute must.

❸ Metropolitan Museum of Art★★★
5th Avenue (at 82nd St.)
☎ 535 77 10
Open Tue.-Thu., Sun. 9.30am-5.30pm, Fri.-Sat. 9.30am-9pm.

Be selective – the eighteen departments of the 'Met' house around 500,000 works of art! The section on Islamic art is excellent, as are the 3,000 European paintings. The Egyptian gallery includes an entire temple shipped from the banks of the Nile, and arms enthusiasts will love the 15,000 or so exhibits from Europe, Asia and America. In 1992, the museum opened its first permanent gallery devoted to the arts of south and south-east Asia. In summer, you can enjoy the garden – there's a marvellous view of the tree tops of Central Park.

❹ Jewish Museum★
1109 5th Avenue (at 92nd St. – between 5th and Madison Ave.)
☎ 423 32 00
Open Mon.-Wed. 11am-5.45pm, Thu. 11am-8pm, Fri. 11am-3pm, Sun. 10am-5.45pm
Entry charge ('pay as you wish' Thu. after 5pm).

With its collections of paintings, sculptures, ceremonial objects, documents, photographs, archaeological artefacts and electronic media materials, this museum communicates the key values, emotions and experiences of the Jewish culture. Many exhibits are from pre-war European synagogues. Each year the museum hosts an exhibition by contemporary artists.

❺ Game Show★
1240 Lexington Avenue (at 83rd St.)
☎ 472 80 11
Open Mon.-Sat. 11am-6pm, Thu. 11am-7pm, Sun. noon-5pm.

For a lively evening with friends, Game Show is one of the best shops for board and other games. Besides the inevitable Monopoly (the American version will impress your friends), Pictionary and the real Hüsker Du, you'll find some that are unusual, intriguing or even a little risqué.

❻ STAR MAGIC★★
1256 Lexington Avenue (bet. 84th and 85th St.)
☎ 988 03 00
Open Mon.-Sat. 11am-7.30pm, Sun. 11am-7pm.
www.starmagic.com

Stargazers of every kind will find all they dream of here, with holograms, crystal balls, prisms, pyramids, telescopes, kaleidoscopes and even freeze-dried ice cream for astronauts! Cyber-fans will also find plenty to keep them happy among the many futuristic objects in techno shades and you can impress your New Age friends by bringing back unusual moonstone or rock crystal jewellery.

And if you're looking for something more testing, there are plenty of puzzles on offer, as well as a department reserved for adult games, such as 'Talk Dirty to Me'.

Around the Frick Collection

Between the rows of private mansions converted into museums on 5th Avenue and the city's showcase of impeccable taste on Madison, you'll find the heart of the New York luxury. Take a stroll in Central Park and admire the view. It's pretty spectacular.

❶ Central Park Wildlife Center★★
Central Park (entrance on 5th Avenue at 64th St.)
☎ 861 60 30
Open Apr.-Oct. Mon.-Fri. 10am-5pm, Sat.-Sun. 10.30am-5.30pm; Nov.-Mar. Mon.-Sun. 10am-4.30pm.

This small and unusual zoo is one of the highlights of the park. The animals live in simulated natural habitats, with polar bears and monkeys among the most fascinating of the species at home here. Don't miss the sea-lions feeding time and the farm animal section. Little ones (and big ones) will love it.

❷ Temple Emanu-El ★★
1 E 65th Street (at 5th Ave.)
☎ 744 14 00
Open every day 10am-5pm, Fri. to 4pm.

With its mixture of oriental motifs and Romanesque-inspired structure, the Temple Emanu-El, the largest reformed synagogue in the United States, is of great architectural interest. The inside, too, is worth coming to see. The imposing nave with its Byzantine ornaments can seat over 2,500 people – more than St Patrick's Cathedral.

❸ MacKenzie-Childs★★
824 Madison Ave. (at 69th St.)
☎ 570 60 50
Open Mon.-Sat. 10am-6pm.

Imagine a Victorian doll's house straight out of *Alice in Wonderland*. As soon as you cross the threshold of this shop, you enter another world. A cage full of birds has pride of place in the middle of a room with walls covered in china. From floor to ceiling, room after room on all three floors is full of surprises, with

tea services, vases, china tiles and picture frames. Just take a look around – it's sure to take you back to your childhood.

❹ Polo Ralph Lauren ★★

867 Madison Avenue (at 72nd St.)
☎ **606 21 00**
Open Mon.-Sat. 10am-6pm, Thu. 10am-8pm, Sun. noon-5pm.

Ralph Lauren spent 14 million dollars turning this former Rhinelander mansion into a shop entirely devoted to chic sportswear, with quantities of English paintings, leather

the largest collection of paintings by Edward Hopper. The temporary exhibitions are always exciting.

❻ The Frick Collection ★★★

1 E 70th Street (between Madison and 5th Ave.)
☎ **288 07 00**
Open Tue.-Sat. 10am-6pm, Sun. 1-6pm.
Entry charge.

An impressive private collection dating from the Renaissance is carefully preserved in this magnificent mansion, which once

The Astor family first made 5th Avenue fashionable back in the 1880s, when they moved here at the level of 65th Street (on the present site of the Emanu-El synagogue). Many celebrities followed suit, including Andrew Carnegie and later the Vanderbilts, moving into the first apartment blocks which were beginning to spring up along the street. Nowadays, the eastern part is the location for a number of very elegant shops, while the museums follow one another in quick succession the length of Central Park.

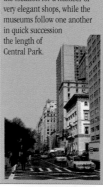

armchairs, oriental carpets and fresh flowers. Skateboard, roller-blade and hip hop enthusiasts are the foremost fans of the 'haute couture' sportswear label, though the clothes themselves might have been borrowed from a New England preppie.

❺ Whitney Museum of American Art ★★★

945 Madison Avenue (at 75th St.)
☎ **570 36 76**
Open Tue.-Thu., Sat.-Sun. 11am-6pm, Fri. 1-9pm.
www.whitney.org

This museum housed in a building designed by Marcel Breuer in 1966 is devoted to modern and contemporary American art. It's the ideal place to discover a host of artists little known outside the United States and to admire

belonged to the industrialist Henry Clay Frick. Every room is sumptuously furnished and hung with works by Rembrandt, Vermeer, Whistler and Renoir. Far from the

large New York museums, which can be a little cold, you'll find a refined, intimate atmosphere. Take a look, too, at the charming garden in the inner courtyard.

Around the Lincoln Center

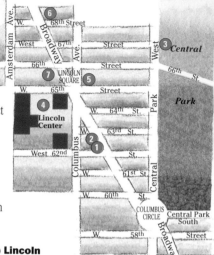

Despite its recent gentrification, this district still has a bohemian side much appreciated by artists and intellectuals. Many showbiz people have moved in, including musicians, actors and pop stars, in search of comfort as well as space.

❶ The Ballet Company ★
1889 Broadway (at 63rd St.)
☎ 246 68 93
Open Mon.-Wed., Fri.-Sat. 10am-6.30pm, Thu. 10am-9pm, Sun 11am-5.30pm.

This tiny shop with its rather kitsch decor is a rare treat for both young dancers and ballet fans alike! It sells tutus, ballet shoes, dancewear, specialised books and videos in the best tradition of the famous New York City Ballet.

❷ Lincoln Stationers ★
1889 Broadway (at 63rd St.)
☎ 459 35 00
Open Mon.-Fri. 9am-8.30pm, Sat. 10am-7pm, Sun. 11.30-6pm.

A marvellous shop, located just next door to the ballet shop that sells not only a variety of art books devoted to the Lincoln Center itself but also an impressive selection of postcards, stationery, pens and fine-quality reproductions of works of art.

❸ Tavern on the Green ★★
Central Park (at W 67th St.)
☎ 873 32 00
Open Mon.-Thu. 11.30am-3pm, 5.30-10.30pm, Fri. 11.30am-3pm, 5-11pm, Sat. 10am-3pm, 5-11pm, Sun. 10am-3pm, 5.30-10.30pm.

The Tavern on the Green is one of Manhattan's landmark restaurants. Overlooking Central Park, it has been serving food to New Yorkers and visitors for almost 25 years and is an endearingly kitsch riot of mirrors and chandeliers. Warner Leroy is in charge, Gary Coyle is the chef, and the cuisine is classic American and very good. It's the place to be seen so book early. The wine list boasts 1,000 labels.

❹ The Lincoln Center ★★★

70 Lincoln Plaza (between 65th St. and Columbus Ave.)
☎ 875 54 56 (customer service)
Guided tour every day 10am-5pm (☎ 875 53 50)
www.lincolncenter.org

The Lincoln Center, built in the 1960s, is a huge complex of performance venues. It's home to the world's most famous opera houses, 'The Met' (☎ 362 60 00, www.metopera.org), and the Avery Fisher Hall (☎ 875 50 30) in which the New York Philharmonic, founded in 1842, perform (www.newyork philharmonic.org). The Library for Performing Arts houses a collection of papers relating to dance, theatre and music. The performances have an excellent reputation and the Lincoln Center is a mecca for music lovers the world over.

❺ American Folk Art Museum ★★

2 Lincoln Square
☎ 595 95 33
Open every day 11am-7.30pm (Mon. to 6pm).
45 W 43rd Street
☎ 265 10 40
Open Tue.-Sun. 10am-6pm, (Fri. to 8pm), closed Mon.

The Folk Art Museum now features highlights of its collection in two magnificent locations, the Eva and Morris Feld Gallery at Lincoln Square and the new building at W 43rd Street. Folk art lies at the heart of American culture and this

❼ Juilliard School of Music ★★

60 Lincoln Center Plaza
☎ 799 50 00
For tours contact the admissions office.

This prestigious school founded in 1905 has numbered several celebrated contemporary tenors, including Philip Glass, among its students, as well as some outstanding soloists, such as Leonard Road and Barbara Hendrix. Dance and theatre are also taught here. The school often stages free concerts and recitals by students and teachers.

museum is devoted to these popular works. The exhibits cover most of the decorative arts (ceramics, fabrics and furniture), as well as cooking utensils and toys. They also stage readings of artists' works, as well as shows, themed events and activities for children.

❻ Loews Cineplex and Imax Theatre ★

1992 Broadway (at 68th St.)
☎ 336 50 00.

This 12-screen cinema boasts a giant Imax screen an incredible eight storeys high. Depending on the film currently showing, you'll experience New York, the ocean depths or the wide African plains, all in dynamic 3D.

Traditional popular art at the Museum of American Folk Art.

Greenwich Village and West Village

Together, Greenwich Village, located at the heart of 'The Village' (between Broadway and 7th Avenue South), and West Village form a leafy residential district with an almost country feel, in strong contrast to the tall buildings that surround it. The pretty pink brick houses of this 'village within a city' combine with the bijoux shops and cafés to give the area a certain bohemian charm. It's home to artists, students and a cast of sometimes unusual-looking characters and is the stronghold of the New York gay community.

the Stonewall Riot of 1969, the Gay Pride parade passes through this spot in June every year.

❶ Sheridan Square ★★

Sheridan Square is a small green space that's home not only to the statue of General Philip Sheridan but also to the lifesize sculpture 'Gay Liberation' by George Segal which depicts two gay couples, male and female, erected in honour of the Gay Rights movement. To commemorate

❷ Condomania ★★
351 Bleecker Street (at 10th St.)
☎ 691 94 42
Open Sun.-Thu. 11am-11pm, Fri.-Sat. 11am-midnight.

This shop aims to put the fun back into safe sex. With condoms of every colour and flavour on offer, including strawberry, chocolate and vanilla, as well as a range of adult gifts, you can bring back something useful and

amusing for your friends – at least those you know very well! The shop also doubles as an Aids information centre.

3 Grove Street ★★

In this charming, tree-lined street far from the hustle and bustle of the city, there are rows of pretty wooden houses dating from the 19th century. The corner of Bedford Street and Grove Street is known as Twin Peaks. Don't worry, though – you won't see any psychopaths bursting out of the building it's named after its double roof.

4 Café Mona Lisa ★★
282 Bleecker Street
(at 7th Ave.)
☎ 929 12 62
Open Fri.-Sat. 11-3am,
Sun.-Thu. 11-2am.

This café, with its neo-Classical decor complete with gilded mirrors, is the ideal place to come for a break after a walk in the Village. Try one of the original salads while comfortably seated in a wing chair covered in sumptuous fabric.

5 Flight 001 ★★
96 Greenwich
Avenue
☎ 691 10 01
Open Mon.-Fri. noon-8pm, Sat. 11am-8pm,
Sun. noon-6pm.

If you're interested in planes or indeed any aspect of travel, this is the shop for you. Classic items such as bags, suitcases, cards and guides are for sale alongside games and gadgets and

anything in miniature that you could imagine or need (or imagine you need) such as creams, toothpaste, razors etc. For those who tremble at the thought of taking to the skies, there's the Fear of Flying Kit with its selection of calming essential oils ($12).

6 Village Chess Shop ★
230 Thompson Street
(between Bleecker St.
and W 3rd St.)
☎ 475 81 30
www.chess-shop.com
Open every day noon-midnight.

The Village Chess Shop, known locally as 'The Chess Shop', has been at the same location since 1972, right in

7 WASHINGTON SQUARE PARK ★★

This is the intellectual and artistic heart of the Village, where you'll come across street entertainers, musicians, chess players, students, hip-hop kids, skaters and poets (and even a few people waiting expectantly for a blind date). The land was given to freed slaves by the Dutch and was then used for military parades. A triumphal arch commemorates the 100th anniversary of the inauguration of George Washington (1892).

the heart of Greenwich Village and just a block down from Washington Square Park. Chess players can choose from hundreds of chess sets, ranging from $5 for a pocket version up to $4,500 for a 15th-century Florentine set complete with bronze pieces, as well as backgammon sets and books. Browse from noon to midnight seven days a week, 365 days a year, or come in and play a game ($1 to play or $3 to watch). David Lee Roth and Yoko Ono are regulars. The more ornate sets feature characters from *Alice in Wonderland*, Shakespeare, *The Simpsons* and *Lord of the Rings*. Beginners can have lessons for $25 an hour.

A stroll through the ethnic neighbourhoods

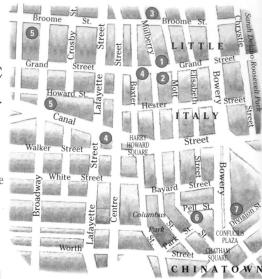

Don't bother to look out for the usual monuments in this district. Just breathe in the exotic aromas of one of the liveliest and most colourful areas of Manhattan. Chinatown is gradually encroaching on Little Italy, long since adandoned by its original Italian inhabitants. There are many places where English isn't even spoken so try not to lose your way.

This cheesemonger's has been in Little Italy for over a century. It's the best place to buy mozarella and ricotta, not to mention the endless varieties of homemade pasta with spinach, tomatoes and cheese. The old recipes of Mama Pina, who founded the shop in 1892, are still in use today.

❶ Alleva Dairy ★★
188 Grand Street
☎ 226 79 90
Open every day 8.30am-6pm.

❷ Ferrara ★★
195 Grand St. (between Mott and Mulberry St.)
☎ 226 61 50
Open Sun.-Fri. 7.30am-midnight, Sat. 7.30-1am.

The oldest espresso bar in the United States, founded in 1892, is also one of the most popular coffee spots in town and has become some-thing of an institution. As well as coffee, it serves a huge variety of delicious Italian pastries, sweets and cookies to eat on the spot or take away. When it's fine, you can sit outside and sample some genuine Italian ice cream.

❸ Umberto's Clam House ★
178 Mulberry Street
(at Broome St.)
☎ 431 75 45
Open every day 11am-4am.

Umberto's Clam House is a first-rate restaurant but it's even better known as the place where 'Crazy Joe' Gallo, one of the godfathers of the Italian mafia, was gunned down in 1972 while celebrating his birthday. This is rather a pity since the fish specialities are good and the wine list interesting. Allow around $25 per person.

❹ Canal Street and Grand Street ★★

Canal Street (between Broadway and Mulberry St.) is well known for being counterfeit kingdom, with faked copies of brands such as Rolex, Cartier and Prada, together with bargain goodies, including perfume. Watch out – these counterfeit items are illegal and could be impounded at customs. The Grand Street market, located between Chrystie and Baxter Streets, has the best fish, vegetables and fruit in New York. Make your way there at the weekend when all the local Chinese residents do their shopping. It's quite an experience.

❺ Pearl River Mart ★★
**277 Canal Street
(at Broadway)
☎ 431 47 70
and 200 Grand Street
☎ 966 10 10
Open every day
10am-7.15pm
www.pearlriver.com**

Pearl River Mart is a gold mine of all things Chinese. The vast space is full of clothes, fabric, crockery, household fabrics, bonsai trees, cosmetics, plant-based remedies and food. The paper lanterns and satin pyjamas ($20-50) are particularly attractive. You're likely to emerge laden with purchases but the prices are very reasonable on the whole, so you shouldn't break the bank.

❼ EASTERN BUDDHIST TEMPLE ★★
**83 Division Street
☎ 226 90 27
Open every day 9am-5pm.**

To find a little Zen serenity in a busy district, go along to this red and gold Buddhist temple. This is where the faithful come to kneel and make offerings to a porcelain statue of Buddha. The less pious can go and take a look around the little shop at the back, where they'll find statuettes, joss sticks and lucky charms of every kind.

❻ Peking Duck House ★★
**22 Mott Street
☎ 227 18 10
Open Sun.-Thu. 11.30am-10.30pm, Fri.-Sat. 11.30am-11.30pm.**

This restaurant certainly deserves the seven stars awarded it by the *Daily News* magazine. Some even consider it the best Chinese restaurant in the world. If someone else is buying, order the famous Peking Duck Extravaganza ($34), which is big enough for two people. Otherwise, try the delicious starters ($5-13) – the prawns with garlic are absolutely delicious. Don't forget your Fortune Cookie at the end of the meal, so you can find out what the future has in store!

Central Park West

This part of the Upper West Side has a more relaxed atmosphere. Students rub shoulders with writers and house-wives, and the streets take on a more human face far from the skyscrapers. Central Park, the essential lungs of the city, makes this residential district full of museums a particularly pleasant place to be.

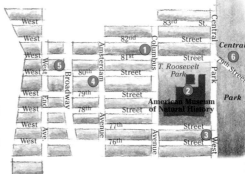

❶ Maxilla & Mandible★★
451-5 Columbus Avenue (between 81st and 82nd St.)
☎ 724 61 73
Open Mon.-Sat. 11am-7pm, Sun. 1-5pm.

Casts of the fossil skulls and bones of various vertebrates (including Homo sapiens) are on sale in this shop, located near the Museum of Natural History. Giant insects are displayed in showcases, side by side with reptiles and other delightful (!) creatures.

For $9, you can treat yourself to a beetle made into a pendant.

❷ American Museum of Natural History★★★
Central Park West (at 79th St.)
☎ 769 51 00 (information)
Open every day 10am-5.45pm (Rose Center is open to 8.45pm Fri.).

The biggest natural history museum in the world occupies over twenty-two buildings that take up four blocks all by themselves.

Around thirty-six million items are on display in a number of sections, including biology, anthropology, ecology and natural science. Most impressive, however, are the dinosaur rooms with their life-size models of dinosaurs and The Rose Center, a planetarium which features displays on the history of the universe. There's also an Imax cinema offering interesting natural science films, as well as temporary exhibitions.

❸ New York Historical Society★★
2 W 77th Street (at Central Park West) ☎ 873 34 00 Open Tue.-Sun. 11am-5pm.

Founded in 1804, this history museum is also the oldest museum in New York. The exhibitions are constantly changing but the permanent collection includes such diverse exhibits as Tiffany lamps, lithographs of Governor Morris's wooden leg and a lock of George Washington's hair! There's even a section devoted to the real Pocahontas popularised in animation by the Walt Disney film.

❹ Allan & Suzi★★
416 Amsterdam Avenue (at 80th St.) ☎ 724 74 45 Open Mon.-Sat. noon-7pm, Sun. noon-6pm.

This vintage clothing store is where most of the top models come to sell their cast-off couture clothes. You can easily find Alaïa or Chanel suits and Mugler or Gaultier evening dresses. They're obviously not giving anything away but there are still good bargains to be had. The clothes are always in

excellent condition and most have only been worn once or twice. The shoe department is fantastic, with a mixture of offbeat and smart traditional styles.

❺ Zabar's★★
2245 Broadway (at 80th St.) ☎ 787 20 00 Open Mon.-Fri. 8am-7.30pm, Sat. 8am-8pm, Sun. 9am-6pm.

Breathing in the aromas coming from this shop you'll quickly understand why the majority of New Yorkers think it's a paradise. Everyone agrees it's the best deli in the city, especially if top-quality fish is what you're looking for. Be sure not to miss the

❻ Central Park★★
Entrances at W 72nd Street, W 77th Street and W 81st Street ☎ 360 27 74 www.centralpark.org

Central Park covers an area of 340 hectares (850 acres) and is a real oasis for New Yorkers, who enjoy jogging, rollerblading, skateboarding or just strolling through it. The terrace of Belvedere Castle (located opposite the American Museum of Natural History) has one of the best views in the city. You can hire a rowing boat from the Loeb Boathouse or

take a trip in a gondola on the lake (☎ 517 47 23). In winter, the Wollman Memorial Rink (at E 64th Street) is the best open-air ice-rink in Manhattan and is impossibly romantic at night. Strawberry Fields, a memorial to John Lennon who lived not far from this spot, is a must for Beatles fans (at West 72nd Street), and the reservoir at W 86th Street will bring back memories of scenes from the film *Marathon Man* for Dustin Hoffman afficionados. In summer a number of enjoyable concerts and open air events take place in the park, as well as walking tours and discovery kits, which will keep children amused for hours (☎ 772 02 10).

kitchen utensil department on the first floor. The prices are very affordable and the products themselves are of excellent quality. Expect to queue, though – it's the price of success.

SoHo

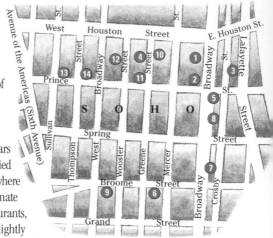

C lassed as a historical area by the City of New York, SoHo (literally 'South of Houston') has in the last few years become a gentrified cultural centre, where art galleries alternate with shops, restaurants, bars and hip, if slightly snobbish, clubs. The warehouses and factories, with their cast-iron frontages and ubiquitous iron fire escapes, have been turned into studios and magnificent lofts. You could spend a good half-day wandering among the shops and galleries.

❶ The Museum for African Art★★

593 Broadway (between Houston and Prince St.)
☎ 966 13 13
Open Tue.-Fri. 10.30am-5.30pm, Sat.-Sun. noon-6pm.
Entry charge.

This quiet little museum was designed by Maya Lin. The main displays, on African or Afro-American art, change about twice a year and the works on show are always of very high quality. The shop in the entrance is especially well stocked with African books and artefacts and there's a section reserved for children.

❷ The New Museum of Contemporary Art★★★

583 Broadway (between Houston and Prince St.)
☎ 219 12 22
Open Tue.-Sun. noon-6pm, (Thu. to 8pm).
Entry charge (half price Thu. 6-8pm).

This museum is entirely devoted to questioning artistic matters and is definitely the most innovative, if not the most controversial, in its field. Many of the works deal with problems of identity, culture, politics or sexuality. Recently enlarged and renovated throughout, the museum has an excellent bookshop specialising in contemporary

art. All in all, it's a fascinating place guaranteed to upset many a preconceived idea.

❸ Pop Shop★★

292 Lafayette Street (between Houston and Prince St.)
☎ 219 27 84
Open Mon.-Sat. noon-7pm, Sun. noon-6pm.

Here you'll find every conceivable object covered with the late Keith Haring's

❹ Kelley and Ping★★
127 Greene Street
☎ 228 12 12
Open Mon.-Sun. 11.30am-11pm.

Kelley and Ping is both a Pan-Asian deli and a restaurant. It specialises in Chinese noodles and rice-based dishes, and the high ceilings and wooden floor give the place a friendly atmosphere and something of the feel of a Shanghai up-market canteen. At lunchtime you can help yourself from the kitchen that opens directly onto the dining area. The noodle soups are particularly tasty and very generous ($7).

and colour – taxis, shells and cartoon characters – served in a designer decor and temptingly presented. Try a delicious espresso from the counter at the entrance.

❻ Modern Stone Age★★
54 Greene Street (at Broome St.)
☎ 219 03 83
Open Mon.-Fri. 10am-7pm, Sat. 11am-7pm, Sun. noon-6pm.

well-known graffiti. Haring himself decorated the entire shop interior from floor to ceiling with his famous little men. Babies have a place of honour here, with layettes signed by the master of the tag, not to mention the T-shirts, patches, magnets, bags and plastic cushions. These obviously aren't being given away free – after all, fame has its price – but they do make amusing little gifts to take home.

Keith Haring in his shop..

❺ Dean & Deluca★
560 Broadway (at Prince St.)
☎ 226 68 00
Open Mon.-Sat. 10am-8pm, Sun. 10am-7pm.

Dean & Deluca's is one of New York's most chic food stores and has a wide selection of teas, coffees, charcuterie, pasta and homemade pastries, all made with the finest, freshest ingredients. You won't be able to resist the cookies which come in every shape

Modern Stone Age has a huge range of decorative items – each made of stone. Every conceivable type of rock or stone has been transformed into a work of art – candle holders, clocks, mirrors and soap dishes. The detail is wonderful and the finished items quite magnificent. The indoor fountains cost around $250 and add a touch of serenity and Zen to the atmosphere. An unusual and fascinating store.

❼ Canal Jean Co. ★
504 Broadway (between Spring and Broome St.)
☎ 226 11 30
Open every day 9.30am-9pm.

Canal Jean Co. has become a cult store and a SoHo institution. Each of the five levels is brimming with clothes and accessories, and you can spend hours browsing through the merchandise and choosing from the hottest club outfits, Army-Navy gear and vintage clothing. The basement has men's streetwear, with sportswear on the ground floor. The first floor has lingerie – men's and women's – and bags of all kinds. On the second floor are the women's clothes and the third floor is devoted to items brandishing the Levi label. If you're cool, you can't miss it.

❽ Steve Madden ★★
540 Broadway (between Prince and Spring St.)
☎ 343 18 0
Open Mon.-Fri. 11am-8pm, Fri.-Sat. 11am-9pm, Sun. 11am-7.30pm.

Don't be surprised if there's a stretch limo parked outside this store. A-list celebs are regulars here and come in search of footwear, whether the style is contemporary 'street' or nostalgic 1960s and 1970s. Platform soles, leather and leopard-skin boots – the designs are young and trendy, bordering on the outrageous, and the prices are pretty reasonable ($70-100).

❾ Jamson Whyte ★★
47 Wooster St. (at Broome St.)
☎ 965 94 05
Open Mon.-Sat. 11am-7pm, Sun. noon-6pm.

Jamson Whyte is one of SoHo's hidden treasures. Housed in a huge loft, this store selling Indonesian furniture and decorative items is a haven of peace in which to escape the hustle and bustle of the streets for a while. The gentle sound of the fountains will calm you down as you admire the fabulous furniture and take a virtual journey to Indonesia. A magnificent bed will set you back around $2,000.

⑩ Moss ★★
146 & 150 Greene Street (at Houston St.)
☎ 226 21 90
Open Tue.-Fri. 11am-7pm, Sat. noon-7pm, Sun. noon-6pm.

This is a design oasis, full of stunning creations by such luminaries as Philippe Starck and Alessi. Moss has an impressive

range of objects for the bedroom, bathroom, kitchen or office, selected from all over the world. The collection includes such varied items as polyurethane vases, large multi-coloured brooms, shelves that seem to move and designs that are (or soon will be) classics. But remember, designer chic doesn't come cheap!

closed mid-June to mid-Sep. Entry free.

This permanent installation, a 360 sq m/3,800 sq ft 'earth sculpture' designed by the conceptual artist Walter de Maria in 1980, certainly won't leave you indifferent – you'll either love it or hate it. Either way, it's a landmark of Land Art, an artistic movement of the 1970s.

⓫ Jerry's★
101 Prince St.
☎ 966 94 64
Open Mon.-Wed. 9am-11pm, Thu.-Fri. 9am-11.30pm, Sat. 10.30am-11.30pm, Sun. 10.30am-5pm (brunch).

This restaurant is a SoHo institution frequented by the entire New York art world. The decor is very 1950s, with its red leatherette seats, while the food is decent and reasonably priced, especially considering the district. Main courses cost between $11-22.

⓬ The New York Earth Room★★
141 Wooster Street (between Prince St. and Houston St.)
☎ 473 80 72
Open Wed.-Sat. noon-6pm (closed 3-3.30pm),

To say any more would only spoil the surprise.

⓭ F.A.I.P. Untitled★
159 Prince Street (at Thomson St.)
☎ 982 20 88
Open Mon.-Sat. 10am-10pm, Sun. 11am-9pm.

⓮ GIRLPROPS. COM★
153 Prince Street (at West Broadway)
☎ 505 76 15
www.girlprops.com
Open every day 10am-10pm (to midnight Fri. & Sat.)

Enter the kingdom of hair accessories and jewellery in this tiny basement shop. Colourful feathers, hair ornaments, feather boas, crystal tattoos, crazy wigs, rings and bracelets – they're all here. It's a pre-teen girl's paradise, and the prices are within budget. They also have an excellent internet store, so you can stock up on your favourite items even when you get home.

This little shop, specialising in fine art in print (hence the name), has been a postcard and art magazine paradise and SoHo landmark since 1970. All the postcards are classified by theme and author so you can easily find what you're looking for. There's also a wide choice of art and design books that you'd have great difficulty finding elsewhere, and even here there's sometimes only a single copy available.

Old postcard of the Brooklyn Bridge.

From Union Square to the Flatiron Building

This district, recently nicknamed 'SoFi' (an abbreviation of 'South of Flatiron') by large numbers of New Yorkers, is becoming more and more fashionable now that a large number of trendy shops and restaurants have moved into the old 19th-century cast-iron buildings.

❶ Flatiron Building ★
175 5th Avenue (at 23rd St. and Broadway).

On the corner of Fifth Avenue and Broadway stands the 21-storey building that ushered in the era of skyscrapers in New York. The Fuller Building, named after its first owners and renamed the Flatiron because of its shape, was built by Daniel H. Burnham in 1902. Its wafer-thin architecture, which was considered very original and innovative at the time, is decorated with steel plates embellished with patterns inspired by the Italian Renaissance.

❷ Otto Tootsi Plohound ★
137 5th Avenue
☎ 231 3199
Open Mon.-Fri. 11.30am-7.30pm, Sat. 11am-8pm, Sun. noon-7pm.

This store is stocked with jewels such as Prada's latest designs, Miu Miu's sporty sneakers and Fantini's orange leather mules. Some of the designs are pretty avant-garde but they are on the New Yorkers' must-have lists and you might spot a celebrity or two trying on shoes here. It's a huge store and the prices can be pretty reasonable.

❸ Union Square Greenmarket ★★
Union Square (at Broadway and 17th St.)
Open Mon., Wed., Fri. and Sat. 8am-6pm.

Old-style markets aren't easy to find in New York and this

7 MOVIE STAR NEWS ★★
134 W 18th Street
☎ 620 81 60
Open Mon.-Sat. 11am-6pm.

Behind this garage hallway lies one of the finest photo and poster shops in New York. It may not be the only shop of its kind in the city, but it's certainly the one with the rarest film posters – Cassavetes, Bunuel, the great classics of the 1940s and 50s, and Russ Meyer – in fact, a gold mine for collectors at very reasonable prices ($10-150).

is one of the best. Dozens of small producers sell their wares here, including fruit, vegetables, bread, cheese, preserves and wine – all of it handmade and guaranteed organic. You can often try the produce before buying it, which is always an advantage. The flower stalls are lovely, too.

4 Urban Outfitters ★★
526 6th Avenue (corner of 14th St.)
☎ 1 646 638 16 46
Open Mon.-Fri. 10am-9pm, Sat. 10am-10pm, Sun. 11am-8pm.

A visit to Urban Outfitters is essential for those visitors to New York who just long to know what everyone is wearing on the streets. The chain is less well known than Gap, but it has a great reputation in America. It sells men's and women's clothes, accessories, books, gadgets and decorative items

for the home – all aimed at a young and trendy market. Be there or be square!

5 ABC Carpet & Home ★★★
888 Broadway (at 19th St.)
☎ 473 30 00
Open Mon.-Fri. 10am-8pm, Sat. 10am-7pm, Sun. 11am-6.30pm.

This store is spread over six floors and is like a museum of interior design and decoration. The stock comes from all over the world and includes fabulous household linen, fabrics and cushions. The third floor is wonderful and looks like an up-market secondhand store, selling everything for babies

and children from furniture, clothes and toys. The far end of the ground floor is home to a number of restaurants in which you can take a welcome rest from shopping.

6 Anthropologie ★★
85 South 5th Avenue
☎ 627 5885
www.anthropologie.com
Open Mon.-Sat. 10am-8pm, Sun. 11am-7pm.

Anthropologie occupies two floors of an enormous loft space and sells women's clothes (at around $170 for a dress and $80 for a skirt), children's outfits, household linen, crockery, home décor, jewellery and a whole range of items that make perfect gifts. The welcoming atmosphere and attractive interior make this a really pleasant place to shop.

TriBeCa

After SoHo, it's the turn of the (Tri)angle (Be)low (Ca)nal Street to be gentrified. Artists and gallery owners have moved into the district's plentiful former industrial premises in the quest for independence.

Robert de Niro has restaurants and a production company in the area. Fortunately, TriBeCa is still a charming oasis just a step away from Wall Street and the financial district.

❶ Screening Room ★★

54 Varick Street (just below Canal St.)
☎ **334 21 00**
Open Mon. 6-11pm, Tue.-Thu. noon-3pm, 6-11pm, Fri. noon-3pm, 6pm-midnight, Sat. 6pm-midnight, Sun. 11am-11pm.

The idea of Screening Room is to combine the three favourite pastimes of New Yorkers – eating, drinking and watching movies. It's a restaurant, bar and movie theatre all in one and comes high on the list of Tribeca's coolest spots. It screens independent or foreign films, with the 'dinner and movie' option priced at $35. Jazz concerts are regularly held in the lounge area, and Sunday brunch followed by the 1.15pm screening of *Breakfast at Tiffany's* is a must for movie fans.

❷ Burrito Bar ★

305 Church Street (at Walker St.)
☎ **219 92 00**
Open every day 11.30am-midnight.

Burrito Bar is a totally psychedelic Mexican restaurant. The front puts you in the picture straight away, with flower frescoes and 'peace & love' symbols in every acid shade. The inside isn't a disappointment either. You'll be able to try a scrumptious *burrito* (a house

such as felt cushions ($120), Leonardo glasses and leather bags by Melanie Dizon (from $330). The collections change regularly, and each month a new designer is introduced. The shop recently expanded and opened a gallery in SoHo (83 Grand Street, ☎ 925 55 06).

❻ LAYLA ★★
211 West Broadway (at Franklin St.)
☎ 431 07 00
Open Sun.-Thu. 5.30-11pm, Fri.-Sat. 5.30-11.30pm.

This restaurant, opened by Robert de Niro and his partners, specialises in Middle Eastern cuisine. The setting is sumptuous and it becomes totally magical in the evening when the stained-glass lamps are lit – you'd think you were in a tale from the *Thousand and One Nights*. De Niro is known to choose his chefs well and the cuisine here is renowned – as are the prices!

speciality), or Mexican soup seated at a 1960s-style table, or leaning against the leopardskin bar.

❸ Totem Design
71 Franklin Street (between Church St. and Broadway)
☎ 925 55 06
Open Mon.-Sat. 11am-7pm, Sun. noon-5pm.

Totem is an acronym for 'the objects that evoke meaning'. This furniture and interior decor shop is decidedly minimalist and sells all the latest designs for the home,

❹ Anandamali ★
35 North Moore Street
☎ 343 89 64
www.anandamali.net
Open Tue.-Sat. 11am-5pm.

Anandamali is housed in a huge loft and is both a shop and a gallery where new exhibitions are regularly held. Cheryl Hazan is the owner and with her talented team she transforms tables, picture frames, cabinets and vases into attractive and functional works of art by applying the mosaic-making technique known as *picassiette*. Fragments of china and ceramics are used to decorate the pieces, and the results are quite stunning (although not cheap at

$1,000 for a round table). The atmosphere is really welcoming and it's a fascinating spot.

❺ Knitting Factory ★★
74 Leonard Street (between Broadway and Church St.)
☎ 219 30 06
www.knittingfactory.com
Open every day 4.30pm-4am.

This is one of Tribeca's institutions, a three-storey alternative music theme park, where you can hear all kinds of sounds, including experimental jazz. Enjoy a coffee or browse through the CDs in the 'Old Office Lounge' from 4.30pm onwards. Come for a drink in the evening and choose from a selection of 18 beers on tap. There are regular concerts, and you can dine while you listen to the coolest new sounds.

Chelsea: a foretaste of the Village

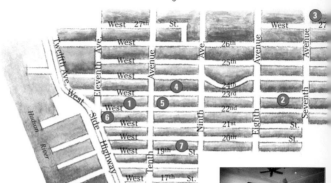

Although Chelsea is renowned for being the haunt of young night-owls, there are still a number of interesting places to visit in the daytime. It's a quiet district, with tree-lined streets and brick houses – in a way, a kind of tranquil foretaste of the Village.

❶ Wild Lily Tearoom ★★

511 W 22nd Street (between 10th and 11th Ave.)
☎ 691 22 58
Open Tue.-Sun. 11am-10pm.

This venue embraces the spirit of Chelsea. It's a restaurant cum tearoom, a little oasis in which to escape the demands of the city. Listen to the gentle rhythm of the warm water fountains or the melodic sounds of opera as you sip a cup of tea (having chosen from over 40 varieties) or enjoy an Asian-style lunch. Dinner comes in the form of tapas-size dishes. Exhibitions of work by young artists and classical music concerts are held in this haven of peace, the perfect place in which to recharge your batteries.

❷ Chelsea Hotel ★★

222 W 23rd Street (between 7th and 8th Ave.)
☎ 243 37 00.

One of the New York's first condominiums, built in 1884, was converted into a hotel in 1905 and became a firm favourite with writers and celebrities such as Mark Twain, Tennessee Williams, Dylan Thomas, Sarah Bernhardt and Arthur Miller. Andy Warhol even made a film (*Chelsea Girls*) here. The rooms are sometimes a little old-fashioned, but the art gallery in the lobby is worth seeing. Suite 303 is now a hair salon where you can get a new look for around $70 (☎ 633 10 11). Remember to check out the unusual motifs on the balconies if you have time.

❸ The Museum at FIT ★★

7th Avenue (at 27th St.)
☎ 217 58 00
Open Tue.-Fri. noon-8pm, Sat. 10am-5pm.

The Museum at the Fashion Institute of Technology has the world's largest collection of costumes and textiles displayed in two public galleries, both devoted entirely to fashion and its history. You'll discover all there is to

know about the huge fashion industry, the way it operates and its different ethnic influences. The creations of many promising new designers are also on display.

❹ London Terrace Apartments ★
Between W 23rd and W 24th St./9th and 10th Ave.

Built in 1930 by Farrar and Watmaugh in a neo-Grecian style, the London Terrace building contains over 1,600 apartments. It may look cold on the outside but the façade is magnificently designed.

❺ Empire Diner ★★
**210 10th Avenue
(at 22nd St.)
☎ 924 00 11
Open 24 hours
(closed Tue. 4-8.30am).**

Empire Diner's 1929 Art Deco chrome decor attracted Andy Warhol back in the 1960s, when he came to buy his sandwiches here. At about the same time, its unusual silhouette was immortalised by the hyper-realist painters. Today, it still has a trendy, artistic clientele, who meet here for a quick meal. The soups are delicious and the choice of sandwiches is very wide (allow $20).

❻ DIA Center for the Arts ★★
**545 & 548 W 22nd Street
(between 10th and 11th Ave.)
☎ 989 55 66
Open Wed.-Sun. noon-6pm,
closed mid June-mid Sept.
Entry charge.**

This warehouse has been converted into a contemporary art centre with five floors of gigantic loft-galleries showing remarkable and often provocative exhibitions. The DIA Center for the Arts was first

❼ Cushman Row ★
406-418 W 20th Street.

Cushman Row, in the historic district of Chelsea, gives a good idea of the district as it was in about 1850, when it was developing. Its grandeur was compromised thirty years later by the building of the overhead railway, which blocked the view and the light of the houses bordering it. The street is nevertheless lined with very simple, elegant houses in the neo-Grecian style (here known as *Greek Revival*). Note in particular the very fine wrought-iron work.

to move into the district and West Chelsea is now becoming as fashionable as SoHo. The DIA opened a huge new museum in Beacon, New York in spring 2003.

East Village, a lively, offbeat district

East Village is an eccentric district, full of young and artistic people. Signs of its creative spirit are everywhere – in the small boutiques brimming with items by new young designers and the wide ranges of secondhand clothes. You'll see some fairly unusual creations being worn on the busy streets. East Village has one of the highest concentrations of bars and restaurants in the whole of Manhattan, and the atmosphere in the evenings is extremely lively.

the construction of new buildings. This green oasis is particularly original with its psychedelic sculpture (around 14 m/46 ft high), made of wood and objects found on the streets, such as toys and fabric. The locals have christened it 'The Christmas Tree of East Village.'

❷ Astor Place Hairstylist, Inc. ★★
2 Astor Place
(near Broadway)
☎ 475 98 54
Open Mon.-Sat. 8am-8pm, Sun. 9am-6pm.

Come and get a new hairstyle at Astor Place Hairstylist, where an army of hairdressers are waiting to give you the cut of your dreams or of your favourite film star (Bruce Willis and John Travolta are

❶ The 6th Street and Avenue B Community Garden ★
Avenue B and 6th Street.
Open Sat. & Sun. 1-6pm.

Community gardens are a surprising phenomenon in a city like New York. The small gardens are looked after by local inhabitants opposed to

regular clients here). They will shave your head for $11. Originality guaranteed. You have to take a ticket and queue because it gets crowded. Fortunately, there's a DJ to help you while away the time.

❸ Mod World ★★
85 1st Avenue
☎ 460 80 04
Open Mon.-Thu. noon-10pm, Fri.-Sat. noon-11pm, Sun. noon-8pm.

This tiny shop represents all that is unusual and eccentric about East Village. Its shelves are laden with decorative items, accessories and

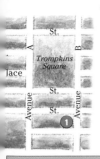

④ Trash & Vaudeville ★★★
4 St Marks Place
☎ 982 35 90
Open Mon.-Thu. noon-8pm,
Fri.-Sat. 11.30am-8pm,
Sun. 1-7.30pm.

⑤ Religious Sex ★★
7 St Marks Place
☎ 477 90 37
Open Mon.-Wed. noon-8pm,
Thu.-Sat. noon-9pm,
Sun. 1-8pm.

⑥ ANDROMEDA ★★
**33 St Mark's Place
☎ 505 94 08
Open every day noon-
8.30pm, Fri.-Sat. 9.30pm.**

If you want to go in for body piercing, you've come to the best place in the district. Ball-closure rings (BCRs), nails and bell-bars are safely and hygienically inserted here. Choose from a wide range of jewellery to put just about anywhere and allow around $45, including insertion. But look out, they say that once you start, you can't stop.

This original shop, run by sales assistants complete with body piercing and tattoos, offers two floors of 1990s-style punk and offbeat accessories, shoes and clothes, including lycra dresses decorated with zips, trash-style check trousers, striped, leopardskin and pop art patterned tights, and metal chain or 1960s-style jewellery. Go and check out the unlabelled, cut-price designer department by names such as Jean-Paul Gaultier.

gadgets, each more surprising than the next. How about a clock made from a cereal packet or a Barbie doll dressed in black leather? You'll just have to investigate for yourself.

It's a misleading name and you'll have to look hard to find this marvellous shop set back from the street, but it's well worth the effort. The trendiest designers have set up a kind of showroom here. The clothes are very expensive but certainly very beautiful and cut from wonderful fabrics, such as silk, velvet and muslin. You're sure to fall in love with the glamorous, low-cut evening dresses that fit like a second skin.

The Lower East Side

The Lower East Side (or 'LES') tells the story of New York's immigrants and the cycle of generations who have moved on to make room for the next. The first immigrants arrived here at the end of the 19th century, and today this popular area is bursting with life and talent. Young designers and artists run and frequent the trendy shops and bars, and you're spoiled for choice on the restaurant front.

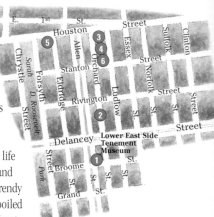

❶ Lower East Side Tenement Museum★★★
90 Orchard Street (at Broome St.)
☎ 431 02 33

Open Tue.-Fri. 1-4pm, Sat.-Sun. 11am-4.30pm.

The reconstructed apartments at this museum allow you to appreciate the conditions in which the mass of immigrants in the 19th century lived. Two have been rebuilt as they were between 1880 and 1935 – one belonging to a Jewish family from Germany and the other to a Sicilian family. The poignant exhibitions and videos highlight the hardship endured by new arrivals in the city. The museum also arranges tours of the district.

❷ Orchard Street Bargain District★
Orchard Street (at Stanton and Delancey St.)

As soon as they arrived, the Jewish immigrants established a thriving textile industry on Orchard Street. They manufactured their own fabrics and garments and sold them from barrows. This spirit of entrepreneurship still lives on today. Several shops sell T-shirts and fabric at great prices. On Sunday, there's a market where you can get some real bargains, but do remember that everything is closed on Saturday.

⑤ IDLEWILD★★
145 E Houston Street (between Eldridge and Forsyth St.)
☎ 477 50 05
Open Tue.-Thu. 8pm-2am, Fri.-Sat. 8pm-4am.

Idlewild is the former name of the JFK airport and this place certainly lives up to its name. Entering the bar is just like boarding an aircraft, and once inside you'll find authentic seats, tables and windows retrieved from a 1960s plane. The waitresses are in stewardess' uniform, of course, so fasten your seat belts and prepare for take off!

❸ Kat'z Deli★★
205 E Houston Street (corner of Ludlow St.)
☎ 254 22 46
Open Sun.-Tue. 8am-10pm, Wed.-Thu. 8am-11pm, Fri.-Sat. 8am-3pm.

Kat'z Deli is one of the most famous in New York, frequented by regulars for decades. The decor has changed little since it was opened in the 1890s, and it still makes about 5,000 lbs of corned beef, 2,000 lbs of salami and 12,000 hot dogs a week – the old-fashioned way, on the premises. The pastrami is wonderful and the Reuben sandwich another favourite. Try an egg dream – a mix of soda, milk and chocolate powder that has become famous since 'that scene' in *When Harry met Sally*.

❹ DDC Lab★
180 Orchard Street (between Houston and Stanton St.)
☎ 375 16 47
Open Mon.-Wed. and Sat. 11am-7pm, Thu.-Fri. 11am-8pm, Sun. noon-6pm.

Described as 'a chemistry set of cool', the white interior and clever shelving of DDC Lab make it a great spot for finding those custom jeans you have always wanted (fitting required) or a Teflon-coated pair with a stretch lambskin

jacket to go with them. Beware, jeans can cost around $200. Browse through the shoes, accessories and cosmetics and then relax with a coffee at the counter, where you can leaf through the latest designer mags.

❻ Lucky Wang★★
100 Stanton Street (between Ludlow and Orchard St.)
☎ 353 28 50
Open Wed.-Sat. 1-7pm, Sun. 1-6pm.
www.luckywang.com

This tiny store is the creation of Emily Wang and Kit Lee. It's a glittering treasure trove of accessories and whacky, clubby clothes, with miniature sparkly bags, fur-covered picture frames and other items in a riot of colours. The perfect spot to find a gift to take home.

Harlem, birthplace of African American culture

Harlem was an infamous no-go area for many years, but all that has now changed. It even has its own tourist office and, what's more, it's the location of Bill Clinton's office. The cradle of African American culture is now an unmissable stop on the itinerary of every New York visitor.

❶ Abyssinian Baptist Church★★
132 W 138th Street
☎ 862 74 74
Open Mon.-Fri. 9am-5pm,
Sunday mass at 9am & 11am.

The Abyssinian Baptist Church was founded in 1808 and contains a museum dedicated to Adam Clayton Powell Jr, the first black man to be elected to Congress (in 1941) and Harlem's representative until 1970. Sunday morning mass is accompanied by a splendid and very moving Gospel choir.

❷ Sylvia's★
328 Malcolm X Bld.
☎ 996 06 60
Open Mon.-Sat.
8am-10.30pm,
Sun. 11am-8pm.

This is the most famous of Harlem's soul food restaurants, with a cuisine deeply rooted in the South (in particular southern California). Sylvia Woods is the godmother of soulfood cooking and has lauched an entire industry, from cookbooks to supermarket produce. Sadly, the venue has become somewhat touristy, but the fried chicken remains an absolute delicacy and the gospel brunch on Sunday is renowned (11am-2pm, beware long queues). There's also a lively jazz brunch on Saturday.

❸ St Nick's Pub★★★
773 St Nicholas Avenue
(corner of 149th St.)
☎ 283 97 28
Open Mon.-Sun. 11am-4pm.

St Nick's Pub is one of the oldest jazz clubs in New York.

It's also one of the rare venues where you can still hear traditional jazz, including be-bop. It's a pleasant setting with a great atmosphere – all in all, a pretty unique spot, where live groups play every evening (except Tuesday) from 9.30pm. Monday evening's jam session is incredible. Jazz lovers shouldn't miss out.

❹ Apollo Theater★
253 West 125th Street
☎ 749 58 38

The focus of 125th Street, this theatre was founded in 1914 as an opera house, exclusively reserved for whites. From 1934 onwards, Frank Schiffman took over the management and turned it into a performance venue that soon became renowned as the best-known showcase for black artists. He started up the

❺ Studio Museum in Harlem★★
144 W 125th Street
(between 7th Ave. and Malcolm X Boulevard)
☎ 864 45 00
Open Wed.-Fri. noon-6pm, Fri. noon-8pm, Sat.-Sun. 1-6pm.

This is America's largest museum dedicated to the work of African-American artists. In addition to its permanent exhibitions, it hosts changing exhibitions and continues its 'artists-in-residence' programme, with a new talent assuming the prestigious position each year.

'amateur nights' that were to launch the careers of James Brown and Sarah Vaughan, among others. Today, this tradition continues on Wednesday evenings from 7.30pm.

❻ Schomburg Center for Research in Black Culture★★
515 Malcolm X Boulevard
☎ 491 22 00
Open Mon.-Wed. noon-8pm, Thu.-Sat. 10am-6pm.

This is the place to come to learn about the history and experiences of peoples of African descent in New York. It's a national research library and cultural conservation

centre, devoted to collecting, preserving and providing access to resources that document black culture.

It also arranges often compelling photographic exhibitions, shows films and hosts concerts (predominantly jazz music).

❼ Hamilton Heights★★
Between 125th and 155th St. (west of St Nicholas Ave.)

This historic district, known as 'Sugar Hill', boasts some of Harlem's most attractive architecture. Stroll along its streets and keep an eye out for

the Hamilton Grange National Memorial (287 Convent Avenue, ☎ 283 51 54), one of New York's oldest buildings. The City College, the 'Harvard of the Poor', commands the contours of Hamilton Heights along with the academic heights of the area and is built of Scottish granite. Constructed between 1903 and 1907, it looks more like a chateau than a university. The main entrance is on the corner of W 138th Street and Convent Avenue. Its alumni include Colin Powell and Martin Scorsese.

Rooms and restaurants
Practicalities

HOTELS

WHERE TO FIND THEM

Hotels are mainly to be found in Midtown, Downtown (around Greenwich Village and SoHo) and Uptown. The southern-most part of Manhattan is home to the business district and financial heart of the city, and is therefore little frequented in the evening. What's more, since 11th September 2001, many of the businesses in this part of the city have remained closed.

to ask about them when making your reservation. For further information, you can contact the Hotel Association of New York (320 Park Avenue, 22nd Floor) on ☎ 754 67 00, www.hanyc.org

RATES AND CONDITIONS

New York is by no means a cheap place to stay. You won't find a decent room under $100 and a room tax of 13.25% will be automatically added to your bill (which adds around $3 per person per night). Rates vary according to the season and often go up over the Christmas and New Year period, for example. Generally speaking, breakfast is not included in the price. Some hotels offer cheap weekend deals so don't forget

RESERVATIONS

If you're going for a long weekend, it's a good idea to book a room in advance. Most of the hotels belong to chains and have free phone numbers (those starting with 1 800 can only be accessed from within the United States), and you can book a room using your credit card. Many can be booked over the internet, which will also allow you to instantly see what rooms and rates are available. It's certainly also possible to make a reservation

once you get to New York, but do bear in mind that a great many conferences take place in the city and rooms can be at a premium during certain periods. There are also certain times when it's vital to book in advance, namely Easter, the week of the New York Marathon (end of October to beginning November), Thanksgiving (end of November) and Christmas.

THE SERVICES OFFERED

A wide variety of services is on offer in New York hotels, but beware, not all of them are free. You may be provided with a coffee machine, hairdryer and free television channels, but a charge is normally made for the use of Nintendo-type video games (keep an eye on your children, the bill can be very steep) and programmable video films. Making a telephone call can also be expensive if you use the phone in your room – each call is subject to hotel tax whether connected or not. Note that the porter who carries your bags to your room will expect a tip of around $1 per bag. If you order room service, it's customary to give a tip of around 15% of the bill to the waiter, unless the service is already included in the price, which is rare in New York.

RESTAURANTS

The food in New York restaurants reflects the diverse cultural and ethnic make-up of the city. With cuisine from all over the world, the gastronomic variety is truly staggering (Chinese, Italian, French, etc. – the list goes on and on). There are restaurants and dishes to suit every pocket, so take the opportunity to try some new ones while you're there. Generally, the meals have three courses – starter, main course and dessert – but it's quite acceptable to order two starters and no main course. Finally, refills of coffee are usually free. It's up to you to say 'when'! You'll find New Yorkers tend to dress quite elegantly for dinner, especially in the smarter restaurants, the men sporting suits and ties, the women chic dresses.

THE RHYTHM OF NEW YORK

Mealtimes in New York follow a familiar pattern. The day begins with breakfast, followed by a light lunch at midday (generally a sandwich or salad since New Yorkers work non-stop). Dinner, on the other hand, is a much more relaxed affair and people take their time over it. New Yorkers tend to dine relatively early on the whole and it isn't unusual for them to arrive at a restaurant at around 6.30pm, which is extremely practical if you're accompanied by young children.

USEFUL INFORMATION

In the summer, a large number of restaurants offer a fixed price lunch ($20), so do make the most of it. Naturally, many places take credit cards, but it's a good idea to check in advance.

Service isn't generally included in the price of meals, but isn't exactly optional either – just remember to add 15% to your bill (20% in luxury restaurants). New Yorkers often simply double the price of the tax – it's much less complicated!

The doggy bags provided by a number of restaurants are an amusing and practical way of avoiding waste. If you don't manage to finish all your meal, you can ask for the leftovers to be wrapped up to take away – after all, you've paid for it and it's yours. Don't be embarassed to ask, Americans ask for doggy bags all the time.

Finally, smokers beware! As of July 2003, smoking is not permitted in bars, restaurants and public buildings, with few exceptions.

IS BOOKING NECESSARY?

It all depends where you want to go, of course. If you decide on a fashionable, elegant or trendy restaurant (such as the Rainbow Room), with a reputation for excellent cuisine, it really is essential to book a table in advance – unless you happen to be lucky and choose a restaurant where the staff will seat you as soon as a table is free. If you have to wait, a cocktail at the bar will help while away the time.

HOTELS

Downtown

The Mercer ★★★

147 Mercer Street
(at Prince St.)
☎ 966 60 60
ⓕ 965 38 38
Subway Prince St.

Opened in 1998 and already very fashionable, the Mercer is a haven of tranquillity. The warm, minimalist decor and furnishings were entirely the work of designer Christian Liaigre. The 75 rooms are very spacious – a luxury in New York – but simple and comfortable. There's even a garden. Prices start at $395, suites from $1,100.

Washington Square Hotel ★

103 Waverly Place
(at MacDougal St.)
☎ 777 95 15
ⓕ 979 83 73
www.wshotel.com
Subway West 4th St.

This hotel, located in the very heart of Greenwich Village,

reflects the district's bohemian charm. The rooms were recently refurbished and the prices are very reasonable (singles $110, doubles $130), and even include continental breakfast. Take a look at the fiery tiled floors of the corridors and restaurant. They were made by Rita Paul, the manager's wife, who has a kiln in the basement.

Best Western Seaport Inn ★★

33 Peck Slip
☎ 766 66 00
ⓕ 766 66 15
Subway Fulton St.

This charming hotel is situated next to South Street Seaport, only a stone's throw from the Brooklyn Bridge. The rooms are decorated in a federal style and some have a terrace, a jacuzzi or even a steam bath.

SoHo Grand Hotel ★★

310 West Broadway
(between Grand and Canal St.)
☎ 965 30 00
ⓕ 965 32 00
www.sohogrand.com
Subway Canal St.

When it opened recently, this was the first new hotel in SoHo since 1880. Celebrities from the worlds of fashion and show business like

its industrial look, which reflects the district's history, and the vast saloon bar is a pleasant place for a late afternoon drink. The only drawback is the small size of the rooms (from $240).

Midtown East

Pickwick Arms ★★★

230 E 51st Street (between 3rd and Lexington Ave.)
☎ 355 03 00
ⓕ 755 50 29
Subway 51st St. or Lexington Ave.

This simple hotel, ten minutes from the Rockefeller Center and 5th Avenue shops, offers really good value for money, with double rooms for $135 and studios (sleeping four) for $130-160 (although most rooms don't have a private bathroom). From the top floor terrace there's a fine view of the city. Clean and quiet, it's opposite a tiny garden in which you can relax.

Four Seasons Hotel ★★★★

57 E 57th Street (between Park and Madison Ave.)
☎ 758 57 00
☎ 758 57 11
Subway 59th St. or Lexington Ave.

FOUR SEASONS HOTEL
New York
A FOUR SEASONS · REGENT HOTEL

Built in a simple, elegant Art Deco style by Pei, the architect who designed the Louvre Pyramid, the Four Seasons is the hotel with the best view of Manhattan. The rooms are very spacious (55 sq m/560 sq ft) and the Florentine marble bathrooms are luxurious. Barely two years after opening, it was named the best hotel in New York by *Traveller* magazine. Rooms from $565 (single) and $615 (double).

Morgans ★★★

237 Madison Avenue (between 37th and 38th St.)
☎ 686 03 00
☎ 779 83 52
Subway Grand Central.

Morgans, designed by Andrée Putman, is one of the finest hotels in New York. Currently very much in vogue, it's appreciated for its stylish decor. Each room has a video player, and there's a gym club and sauna available to guests. Rooms range from $250 to $500.

Gramercy Park ★★

2 Lexington Avenue (at E 21st St.)
☎ 475 43 20
☎ 505 05 35
Subway 23rd St.

Situated near the last privately-owned square in New York, Gramercy Park Hotel is a surprisingly calm and relaxing place. The rooms are no longer

particularly modern but they're comfortable just the same (prices from $160). Some rock and show biz stars come here for a little peace and quiet.

Midtown West

Algonquin ★★★

59 W 44th Street (between 5th and 6th Ave.)
☎ 840 68 00
☎ 944 14 19
www.thealgonquin.net
Subway 42nd St.

This is one of the favourite meeting-places of the cinema, literary and art worlds. The Algonquin is a famous hotel which preserves old European charm in a turn-of-the-century

building. Each floor is a different colour and the rooms are tastefully furnished (from $199). A comfortable hotel with an excellent terrace restaurant.

Royalton ★★★

44 W 44th Street (between 5th and 6th Ave.)
☎ 869 44 00
☎ 869 89 65
Subway Grand Central.

The interior, given a fabulously creative makeover by Philippe Starck, is reminiscent of the Paramount Hotel (p. 72) – the atmosphere is very similar despite the difference in price (rooms from $275 to $500). The restaurant, bar and lounge are all highly regarded and Starck's imaginative bathrooms are amongst the most original in New York.

Best Western Manhattan Hotel ★

17 W 32nd Street
☎ 736 16 00
☎ 563 40 07
www.bestwesternnewyork.com
Subway 34th St.

The rooms were recently renovated and each has a different theme. You can choose between a highly sophisticated 5th Avenue-type decor or the more modern, trendy style of SoHo. There's a very fine hall decorated entirely in black and white, with a series of photos of New York. Very good value for money (from $140 to $250) when you consider that the hotel is situated close to the Empire State Building, as well as being remarkably well served by the subway.

Paramount Hotel ★★

235 W 46th Street
☎ 764 55 00
🅕 354 52 37
www.paramounthotel
newyork.com
Subway 49th St.

Currently all the rage in New York, everyone dreams of spending at least one night in the Paramount Hotel. Designed by Philippe Starck for Ian Schraeger, it's recognisable from

A sumptuous room at the Franklin hotel.

the outside by its grey marble walls adorned with red roses. There are copies of Vermeer paintings on the headboards and fresh flowers in every room. A fashionable hotel offering rooms from around $150 to $400. Many services add to the charm of this reasonably priced high-class hotel.

Shoreham ★★★

33 W 55th Street
(at 5th Ave.)
☎ 247 67 00
🅕 765 97 41
Subway 5th Ave. or 33rd St.

A hotel whose decor makes a change from the traditional floral wallpapers, it's decorated

in black and white throughout. The rooms (from $209) are all elegant, modern and spacious. Continental breakfast is included in the price, which is quite uncommon in New York.

Broadway Inn

264 W 46th Street
(on the corner of 8th Ave.)
☎ 997 92 00
🅕 768 28 07
www.broadwayinn.com
Subway 42th St.-8th Ave.

An unpretentious little hotel with a cosy bed and breakfast-style reception right next to Times Square, Broadway and an endless choice of restaurants. The staff are helpful and the prices moderate, with single rooms $99 and doubles from $139, including breakfast. What more could you want?

Upper East Side

Franklin ★★★

164 E 87th Street (between 3rd and Lexington Ave.)
☎ 369 10 00
🅕 369 80 00
www.franklinhotel.com
Subway 86th St.

A charming little hotel located near the museums of the East

The hall at the Empire Hotel.

Side in a district filled with restaurants. Many top models from the Elite and Ford agencies stay here (probably because the bathrooms are very spacious). The rooms are all modern, comfortable and very practical, all for a reasonable price, with prices from $229. Breakfast and parking included.

Wales ★★

1295 Madison Avenue
(at E 92nd St.)
☎ 876 60 00
🖷 860 70 00
www.waleshotel.com
Subway 96th St.

A quiet, elegant hotel with a turn-of-the-century European air, situated in the attractive historic district of Carnegie Hall. The staff here are very welcoming and you can take afternoon tea in a little drawing-room, where a harpist or pianist sometimes performs. This oasis of peace comes at a reasonable price as well, with rooms starting from $255.

Barbizon ★★★

140 E 63rd Street
(at Lexington Ave.)
☎ 838 57 00
🖷 888 42 71
www.melrosehotel.com
Subway Lexington Ave.

For over fifty years, this hotel was exclusively reserved for emancipated young women. Parents felt secure in the knowledge that their daughters were staying somewhere that Grace Kelly, Ali McGraw and Candice Bergen, among others, had stayed before them. In the autumn of 1996, the Barbizon was renovated at a cost of 40 million dollars and the rooms (now for both sexes) are luxurious. Double rooms from $250.

Upper West Side

The Mayflower Hotel on the Park ★★

15 Central Park West
(at 61st St.)
☎ 265 00 60
🖷 265 02 27
www.mayflowerhotel.com
Subway Columbus Circle.

Some of the rooms (singles $200-240, doubles $225-265) overlook Central Park, so don't forget to ask for one when reserving. Jack Nicolson, Alec Baldwin and Jane Fonda are among the regulars here, as are Placido Domingo and Luciano Pavarotti, who also frequent the hotel bar and restaurant. These are much sought after for their breathtaking views of Central Park, as well as the excellent brunch.

The Empire Hotel ★★

44 W 63rd Street
(at Broadway)
☎ 265 74 00
🖷 315 03 49
www.empirehotel.com
Subway Columbus Circle.

The Empire is perfectly situated opposite the Lincoln Center. The rooms are quite small but tastefully furnished (singles or doubles $200-300, suites $300). The sumptuous hall is worth a look, with two oil paintings, one of Lady Macbeth and another of Laurence Olivier as Romeo, which blend with the velvet drapes and panelling.

RESTAURANTS

Downtown TriBeCa

Nobu ★★★

105 Hudson Street
(at Franklin St.)
☎ 219 05 00
Subway Franklin St.
Lunch: Mon.-Fri.
11.45am-2.15pm
Dinner: every day 5.45-
10.15pm.

Robert de Niro decided to move
into the TriBeCa district by
opening several restaurants here,
including Nobu, for which he
chose one of the best
Japanese chefs. The setting is
sober and elegant and the
dishes live up to the owner's
reputation. The cuisine is first
rate but very expensive. You need
to bank on spending at least $70.

TriBeCa Grill ★★

375 Greenwich Street
(at Franklin St.)
☎ 941 39 00
Subway Franklin St.
Lunch: Mon.-Fri.
11.30am-3pm
Dinner: Mon.-Thu. 5.30-
11pm, Fri.-Sat. 5.30-
11.30pm, Sun. 5.30-10pm
Brunch: 11.30am-2.45pm.

This time De Niro encouraged
fellow-actors such as Sean Penn
and Christopher Walken to
invest in the TriBeCa Grill, a
restaurant serving American
nouvelle cuisine. The clientele
is quite smart and the stars and

their friends often meet at the
bar. That might make it worth
the price (around $45).

SoHo

Balthazar ★★

80 Spring Street
(near Broadway)
☎ 965 14 14
Subway Spring St.
Open every day 7.30am-
midnight (Fri. & Sat. to 2am).

Since its opening in 1997, this
has been the most fashionable
restaurant in New York, with
Madonna, Uma Thurman and
the Baldwin brothers among its
customers. It serves unsurprising
but high-quality dishes in the
attractive setting of a Parisian
brasserie. The large seafood
tray (around $56 for two) is a
must. Balthazar is constantly
packed so try breakfast, which is
pleasant and less frenetic.

Cub Room Café ★★

131 Sullivan Street
(at Prince St.)
☎ 677 41 00
Subway Spring St.
Lunch: Tue.-Fri.
noon-2.30pm
Dinner: Mon.-Fri. 6-11pm,
Sat. 5.30pm-midnight,
Sun. 5.30-10.30pm.

A restaurant serving one of the
finest American cuisines in a
modern urban setting. After it
opened, it quickly became very
fashionable. All the dishes are
prepared using fresh farm
organic produce, a detail much
appreciated by New York diners.

Savoy ★★★

70 Prince Street
(at Crosby St.)
☎ 219 85 70
Subway Spring St.
Lunch: Mon.-Sat. noon-3pm
Dinner: Mon.-Thu.
6-10.30pm, Fri.-Sat.
6-11pm, Sun. 6-10pm.

A warm romantic atmosphere
and light wood decor make this
modest-sized restaurant one of
the most attractive in the SoHo
district. Modest ingredients
are combined to create dishes
with strong, original flavours.
In winter, the log fire is very
welcoming. On the first floor, the
Chef's Dining Room serves a

different meal every day according to what's on offer at the market (around $40).

Honmura An ★★★

170 Mercer Street (between Prince and Houston St.)
☎ 334 52 53
Subway Prince St. or Broadway-Lafayette
Lunch: Wed.-Sat. noon-2.30pm.
Dinner: Tue.-Sun. 6-10pm.
Closed Mon.

If sushi isn't really your cup of tea, Honmura An is ideal – a Japanese restaurant specialising in home-made noodles cooked in a thousand and one different ways. The decor is traditional, elegant and light – a veritable Zen atmosphere. The average cost of a meal is $45.

Lucky Strike ★★

59 Grand St. (between Wooster St. and W Broadway)
☎ 941 04 79
Subway Canal St.
Open Sun.-Wed. noon-3am, Thu.-Sat. noon-4am.

Where do models go to relax away from the catwalk? To the Lucky Strike, of course. Since it opened a few years ago, well-known personalities from Giorgio Armani to Claudia Schiffer have made a beeline for this restaurant serving simple

American and European dishes, with burgers, steaks au poivre, sauté potatoes, etc. (average cost $27). DJ from 11pm onwards.

Little Italy and Chinatown

Angelo's of Mulberry St. ★★★

146 Mulberry Street (between Grand and Hester St.)
☎ 966 12 77
Subway Canal St.
Open Tue.-Thu. noon-11.30pm, Fri. & Sun. noon-12.30am, Sat. noon-1am.
Closed Mon.

For many of Little Italy's restaurants, the cuisine comes second to the picturesque decor. Angelo's is a rare exception. It's an Olde New York-style spot, which owes its excellent reputation to good, traditional southern Italian cuisine, with its characteristic tomato sauce, chillis and olives. The pizzas are delicious.

House of Vegetarian ★★

68 Mott Street
☎ 226 65 72
Subway Canal St.
Open every day 11am to 11pm.

A Chinese vegetarian paradise, which makes a welcome change from the usual healthfood

佛有緣素食館
HOUSE OF VEGETARIAN
68 Mott St. (Bet. Canal & Bayard)   (Chinatown)
New York, N.Y. 10013   Tel: (212) 226-6572

restaurants. You'll think you're eating beef, chicken or fish, yet everything here is based on soya or wholemeal wheat – a great idea for those who are finding it difficult to get used to meatless cookery. Try the *Lo Mein*, with three kinds of mushrooms ($6.75), or the delicious lotus-blossom ice creams ($2).

Greenwich Village

Lemongrass Grill ★★

37 Barrow Street (at 7th Ave. South)
☎ 242 06 06
Subway Christopher St.
Open Mon.-Thu. noon-10.30pm, Fri.-Sat. noon-11.30pm, Sun. 1-10.30pm.

The Lemongrass Grill is a branch of a very popular chain of Thai restaurants, which often get very crowded, so prepare yourself for a queue. The decor is warm and soothing, the food excellent value (around $11 for a main course) and the portions are huge (so huge you could easily share a dish with a friend). The choice is pretty amazing, too. It's a bit of a must in these parts.

French Roast ★★★★

78 West 11th Street
(at 6th Ave.)
☎ 533 2233
Subway W 4th St.
Open 24 hours

Despite its name, French Roast is an American restaurant, located right at the heart of Greenwich Village. The food is excellent and good value and, what's more, it never closes.

Midtown

21 ★★★

21 W 52nd Street
(between 5th and 6th Ave.)
☎ 582 72 00
www.21club.com
Subway Rockefeller Center
Open Mon.-Fri. noon-
2.30pm, 5.30-11.30pm
(Fri. to 11.30pm),
Sat. 5.30-11.30pm.

In the 1950s, this restaurant was reputed to be the meeting-place of such notaries as Dali, Bogart and Hemingway. Chef Erik Blauberg fuses classic American

cuisine with modern innovation. 21 has an award-winning wine list and was recently described by the *New York Times* as a quintessential New York experience. You'll need to allow around $70.

Lespinasse ★★

St Regis Hotel, 2 E 55th
Street (at 5th Ave.)
☎ 753 45 00
www.stregis.com
Subway 5th Ave.
Open Mon.-Sat. 5.30-10pm.

One of the few places in the city to have been awarded four stars by the *New York Times*. From the magnificent decor and impeccable service to the elegant presentation and delicious cuisine, everything about this restaurant is quite superlative. The chef, Christian Delouvrier, prepares a distinctive 'cuisine de terre' and the chief pâtissier, Patrice Caillot, makes delicious and original pastries (gourmet set meal $130).

Uptown Upper West Side

Picholine ★★

35 W 64th Street
(Central Park West)
☎ 724 85 85
Subway 66th St.-
Lincoln Center
Lunch: Tue.-Sat.
11.45am-2pm
Dinner: Mon.-Wed.
5.15-11pm, Thu.-Sat.
5.15-11.45pm,
Sun. 5-9pm.

Picholine takes its name from a small Italian olive. The Mediterranean-inspired cuisine

picholine

here is very original, with many tempting specialities. Try the grilled octopus with fennel or spiced Moroccan lamb. There's an excellent wine list, and the cheeseboard, with cheeses from all over the world, is considered the best in New York. *The* place to stop before a concert at the Lincoln Center. You'll spend around $60 on a good meal.

A MEAL WITH A VIEW

Restaurants and bars in skyscrapers or at the top of buildings offer an unbeatable view over Manhattan.

Top of the Tower
Beekman Tower Hotel
3 Mitchell Place (26th Floor)
(between 1st Ave. and 49th St.)
☎ 355 73 00
Subway 51st St. or Lexington Ave.-3rd Ave.
Open Fri.-Sat. 5pm-2am, Sun.-Thu. 5pm-1am.
Fabulous cuisine, fabulous views., fabulously romantic.

Nirvana
30 Central Park South
Penthouse (59th St. between 5th and 6th Ave.)
☎ 486 57 00
Subway 7th Ave. or Columbus Circle
Open every day noon-1am.
Asian food with live sitar music and fortune tellers.

The View
(Marriott Marquis Hotel)
1535 Broadway.
(between 45th and 46th St.)
☎ 704 89 00
Subway 42nd St.-Times Square
Open Mon.-Thu. 5.30-10.45pm, Fri.-Sat. 5-11.45pm.
Revolving rooftop reataurant and lounge. A little touristy.

Carmine's ★★★

2450 Broadway (between 90th and 91st St.)
☎ 362 22 00
Subway 86th St.
Open Sun.-Thu. 11.30am-11pm, Fri.-Sat. 11.30am-midnight.

The ideal place for people with big appetites, this restaurant serves home-made Italian dishes in enormous portions,

Park Avenue Café.

large enough for three, with such delights on the menu as meatballs and pasta, aubergines with parmesan, broiled steak, four pasta special and tiramisu. The atmosphere is warm and friendly too.

Upper East Side

Aureole ★★★

34 E 61st Street (between Madison and Park Ave.)
☎ **319 16 60**
Subway Lexington Ave.
or 59th St.
Open Mon.-Fri. noon-2.30pm, Sat. 5-11.30pm.

Charles Palmer's romantic restaurant occupies two floors of a house on the East Side, and is an oasis of peace and quiet. The service is excellent and the menu is always surprising and very appetising, especially the chef's delicious starters. Excellent value for money (lunch around $32, dinner $96). Remember to book a table in the garden if you have the time.

Park Avenue Café ★

100 E 63rd Street
(at Park Ave.)
☎ **644 19 00**
Subway Lexington Ave.
Lunch: Mon.-Fri. 11.30am-2.30pm
Dinner: Mon.-Thu. 5.30-11pm, Fri.-Sat. 5.30-11.30pm, Sun. 5-10.30pm
Brunch: Sun. 11am-2.30pm.

The two rooms of this lovely restaurant are decorated with old toys and superb American craft objects, which change according to the owner's purchases. The setting is worthy of the excellent and imaginatively presented eclectic US cuisine served here. Don't miss the delicious desserts, which are the work of chef Richard Leach. Allow around $55 per person.

New York has long been the shopping capital of the world, and temptations lie in wait for you all over the city, in smart shops and street corner markets alike. As in many big cities, every district has its speciality.

SHOPPING

Luxury goods

The luxury shops, such as Saks Fifth Avenue and the celebrated jewellers, Tiffany's, can be found on 5th Avenue and Madison Avenue (between 58th and 49th St.). The windows of Tiffany's are well worth a look.

Macy's, the biggest department store in the world, is on 34th Stteet (at Broadway). In the same area, you can stock up on CDs and find the sneakers of your dreams in one of the VIM chain of stores (34th St. and 5th Ave.). On Broadway, at the level of the Flatiron Building, sportswear enthusiasts will find a good range of shops to suit their every need.

Gadgets, fashion and design

Greenwich Village, 'the Village', has a typical New York atmosphere but, with no skyscrapers, it's also more peaceful. You'll find plenty of gadget, clothes and interior design shops. Some of them are fairly whacky but most are quiet and refined. It's the ideal place to go for an unhurried stroll if you're looking for original little gifts to take home.

Hi-fi and photo

For those in the know, the bazaars of Canal and the neighbouring streets are an endless mine of inexpensive ideas for hi-fi accessories, photography, bags and cases (see Compatability and Voltage, p. 81).

CDs and clubwear

A very specialised clientele throngs the record shops of the West Village on the lookout for the latest house and techno releases. The clothes shops in the surrounding area naturally cater for this influx and bright colours, body piercing, tattoos and dyed hair are the order of the day.

Jeans and streetwear

SoHo has become the melting pot of sportswear and streetwear fashions.

This is the place to come for trendy, sophisticated creations by a new generation of young designers.

NIGHTLIFE

If you'd like to see a musical or a play, the place to go is Times Square with its many theatres (42nd St. and Broadway).

If you feel like dancing all night, head for the East Village. The four dance floors of Webster Hall (11th Street) will ensure that you can boogie to your heart's content.

Greenwich Village is the mecca for jazz, with the two most famous clubs in New York: the Village Vanguard and the Blue Note, which never seem to go out of fashion.

Finally, in SoHo, you have a choice between SOB's, which features a programme of world music, and one of the many late bars.

FINDING THE WAY

You can locate the shops, department stores, bars, cafés, theatres, nightclubs and concert halls described in the Shopping (pp. 82-113) and Nightlife (pp.116-125) chapters of this guide on the map opposite by their letters and numbers (e.g. B3).

 Where to shop

 Nightlife

Shopping Practicalities

New York is the retail and wholesale capital of the US, with countless department stores, small specialised outlets and luxury stores. This is really only to be expected in a city that is both the financial centre of the world and its third largest port, and you should have no difficulty in finding whatever you're looking for. However, do be aware that there are fakes and stolen goods about, so choose your vendor wisely.

January and July sales are something of an institution, but those taking place at other times of year also offer worthwhile reductions, including the sales around Thanksgiving (4th Thu. in November), President's Day, or the last weekend in February (great for clothes and winter sports equipment). The sales which offer the best reductions, however, are those in the department stores.

HOW TO PAY
Traveller's cheques
These are very widely used and accepted by most shopkeepers, so it isn't always necessary to change them into dollars. In many cases you'll be given change in cash. Make sure you record the numbers in case they get lost or stolen. To change traveller's cheques try:

Cheque Point USA
22 Central Park South-59th Street (between 5th and 6th Ave.), ☎ 750 24 00.

Credit cards
As well as being a widespread and practical way of paying for just about anything, credit cards (the most common in

PRICE TAGS
The prices are always displayed in shops but you could be in for a shock when you come to pay if you forget the sales tax. To work out the real cost of an article, you need to add the state tax, which is 8.25% in New York (but 4% on books and 15.25% for hotels). Due to a recent change in the law, you don't have to pay tax on clothes under $100 and there's no tax on goods purchased in duty-free shops at the airports.

BARGAINING
Although you can, of course, always pay the price shown on the label, bargaining is a very common practice in New York, especially in electronics, hi-fi, photographic, gadget and secondhand shops. If you have the time and inclination, it's a good idea to begin by comparing competitors' prices before bargaining with the shopkeeper. If you offer to pay cash, you can often save yourself the tax.

SALES
Sales are more frequent and numerous in the US than in Europe. You can check when sales are taking place by looking in newspapers. The

the US are Visa, American Express and Mastercard) are essential when reserving theatre, cinema or concert seats and hotel rooms. They can also be used as deposits when hiring cars. You can obtain cash using a credit card from almost all cash machines (ATMs), however, a fixed charge is levied on every transaction. Rather than drawing out several small sums of money, it's more economic to withdraw larger sums less frequently. The maximum withdrawal amount varies according to your credit card.

FINDING YOUR WAY

Next to each address in the Shopping and Nightlife and tours sections we have given its location on the map of New York on pages 78-79.

Banks are open Monday to Friday, 9am to 3pm, although some stay open later Thursday evenings. If you need cash outside these hours, there are plenty of cash machines about (ATMs), but use discretion when using one as you are exposed outside.

CUSTOMS DUTY

Make sure you're aware of the duty-free limits imposed when returning home. In the UK you can import a maximum of 200 cigarettes, 100 cigarillos, 50 cigars or 250g tobacco; 2 litres

of still table wine; 1 litre of spirits or strong liqueurs over 22% volume or 2 litres of fortified or sparkling wine or other liqueurs; 250cc/ml of toilet water or 60cc/ml of perfume and £145 worth of all other goods including gifts and souvenirs. You should declare anything in excess of these amounts. Note that if you import a single item worth over £145 you'll have to pay tax on its full value, not just the value in excess of £145. You should also be aware that it's illegal to import pirate copies or fake goods.

COMPATABILITY AND VOLTAGE

Depending on what you buy, you may experience compatability problems using some US products at home. Items to watch out for are anything electrical or related to TV or video, including video cassettes and DVDs. As well as having differently shaped plugs, US electrical products run off 110v (as opposed to 220-240v in the UK). What's more, US TV and video uses a different system, so UK TVs will not work with standard US equipment. US DVD disks won't work unless you own a 'multi-region' player (which are virtually unheard-of in the US!), and only fairly recent video players can cope with US tapes. Computer software, CDs and home telephones are generally fine, however, but avoid buying mobile phones, which work on a different system. If in doubt, consult a reliable salesperson.

KEEP YOUR EYES OPEN!

It's easy to get carried away, but make sure you buy from reputable dealers and be wary of anything that seems like a bargain. Be extra vigilant when it comes to photographic and hi-fi equipment, electronics and imitations of well-known brands. Most of the dubious shops are in the vicinity of 42nd Street. Go and take a look at them by all means, but don't be tempted to buy anything except gadgets. Generally speaking, it's vital to get a receipt as you may be asked to produce it at customs and it will be useful anyway should you ever wish to sell your purchase or need to fill in an insurance claim form after a burglary.

OPENING TIMES

New York is a city that never sleeps, which means many of the stores never close. Shops generally open Monday to Saturday 9.30am to 6pm and stay open until 9pm once or twice a week (usually Thursday evenings). Some shops, such as those in the vicinity of Wall Street, open as early as 7.30 or 8 in the morning but are closed at the weekend. Many branches of the big chain stores, such as **Barney's** and **The Wiz**, stay open until late at night. On the other hand, most shops close early on Saturdays (around 5 or 5.30pm). You'll almost certainly want to spend part of your Sunday in the city shopping, too, as almost all the shops stay open, although Sunday opening hours are rather more restricted than those during the week (from about noon to 6pm).

WOMEN'S FASHION

New York is the fashion and design capital of the United States. The great couture houses are all concentrated on Madison and 5th Avenue, while the trendy and offbeat young designers have shops in SoHo, the Lower East Side or the latest fashionable district, NoLiTa ('North of Little Italy'). Top American fashion designers, such as Donna Karan, Bill Glass and Anne Klein, also have outlets in the department stores.

Anna Sui
113 Greene Street (B3)
☎ 941 84 06
Subway Prince St.
Open Mon.-Sat.
11.30am-7pm, Sun.
11.30-6.30pm.

Anna Sui has become the darling of SoHo. Top models and stars come here to shop for reasonably-priced clothes ($100-150 for a dress). A charming little boudoir with black velvet covered walls (and fabulous changing rooms) is the setting for trendy, avant-garde clothes made of luxurious fabrics (velvet, silk, moiré, etc.), as well as a selection of shoes and a few accessories, such as her well-known bags.

Betsey Johnson
138 Wooster Street
(between Prince and Houston St., B3)
☎ 995 50 48
Subway Prince St.
Open Mon.-Sat. 11am-7pm (Thu. to 8pm), Sun. noon-7pm.

You'll be dazzled by the pink neon and fluorescent lights of

this original, sexily-decorated shop in which Betsey Johnson sells her amazing designs, each more flamboyant and glamorous than the last. Velvet, leather, imitation fur and knitted fabrics are the favourite materials of this designer, and a beautiful embossed velvet dress sells for around $100.

Banana Republic
89 5th Avenue
(at 17th St., B3)
☎ 366 46 30
Subway: 14th St. or 6th Ave.
Open Mon.-Fri. 10am-9pm, Sat. 10am-8pm, Sun. 11am-7pm.

This is Gap's sophisticated sister company, selling practical clothes for men and women in lovely fabrics and flattering styles. There's a huge selection of T-shirts, and the cashmere designs are very feminine and flattering. The decor is classic and streamlined and the presentation attractive – all in all, you are unlikely to emerge empty-handed.

DKNY
655 Madison Avenue
(on corner of 60th St., B1)
☎ 223 35 69
Subway: Lexington Ave.
or 59th St.
Open Mon.-Sat. 10am-7pm (Thu. to 9pm), Sun. noon-6pm.

The DKNY store is a must for fans of the ultra famous New York designer. There are three floors and among the wonderful designs you'll find (expensive) evening dresses, jeans, shoes and accessories. There's a pleasant café in which to choose from an array of fruit juices and fresh vegetables.

Patricia Field

10 E 8th Street
(near 5th Ave., B3)
☎ 254 16 99
Subway 8th St.
Open Sun.-Wed. noon-8pm,
Thu.-Sat. noon-9pm.

Patricia Field is the Vivienne Westwood of New York. When you enter her ultra-trendy shop, you'll be greeted by people wearing the most outrageous and ambivalent clothes – both for men and women. The clothes for sale are quite amazing, constantly changing and reputedly of excellent quality, and there's a wide selection of equally stunning jewellery, too.

Bloomingdale's

100 3rd Avenue (between
59th and 60th St., B2)
☎ 355 59 00
Subway 59th St.
Open Mon.-Thu. 10am-
8.30pm, Fri. 10am-10pm,
Sat. 9am-10pm, Sun. 11am-
7pm.

Founded in 1886, Bloomingdale's is a New York shopping heaven. The store is smaller than Macy's, but is more chic and comprehensive. You'll find everything your heart desires. Models parade around wearing the latest collections on the designer floor, just to make it harder to resist indulging. Calvin Klein and DKNY have their own impressive dedicated spaces.

Henri Bendel

712 5th Avenue (between
55th and 56th St., B2)
☎ 247 11 00
Subway 59th St.
Open Mon.-Fri.
10am-8pm,
Sat. 10am-7pm,
Sun. noon-6pm.

The most luxurious women's clothes store in New York. It's organised as a number of small shops arranged round a central atrium. The make-up department offers a very wide choice of products. Even if you're not buying, it's still a pleasure to look at. Don't miss the upper floor windows designed by René Lalique in 1912. There's also a very elegant tea room.

GAP

60 W 34th Street
(at Broadway, A2)
☎ 760 12 68
Subway 34th St.
Open Mon.-Fri. 9am-9pm,
Sat. 10am-9.30pm,
Sun. 11am-midnight.

Check out the wide range of styles available at GAP at very reasonable prices. With sportswear, casual wear, jackets, sweaters, jeans (from $50), evening dresses (from $70), belts and shoes on offer, you're almost sure to find something you like. GAP also sells clothes for children (Baby GAP and GAP Kids), as well as for men.

Cynthia Rowley

550 7th Avenue,
Floor 19
(at W 36th St., A2)
☎ 575 90 20
Subway Prince St.
Open Mon.-Sat.
11am-7pm,
Sun. noon-6pm.

The 1950s-60s decor of this little shop is a perfect setting for the trendy clothes and retro accessories. Glamorous dresses and hipster trousers in acid shades, leopardskin and pop art handbags, 1950s-style satin shoes and matching hats are all shown to advantage and the prices aren't too steep, especially at sale times. Evening dresses from $200.

CLOTHES SIZES

Don't forget US sizes may be different to those you are used to. See the conversion tables on p. XV of the colour pages for help, so you'll be guaranteed to look a million dollars in that new outfit!

FASHION ACCESSORIES

New Yorkers are mad about fashion accessories, from the most traditional to the most extravagant, that brighten up or personalise an outfit. On every street corner you'll come across a shoe, hat or jewellery shop. Some hold real treasures combining creativity, originality and good quality.

SHOES

John Fluevog

250 Mulberry Street (B3)
☎ 431 44 84
www.fluevog.com
Open Mon.-Fri. 11am-7pm,
Sat. noon-6pm.

Located in the heart of NoLiTa, John Fluevog's shoe store is quite magnificent. If you're looking

for something rather avant-garde and unusual but still elegant, this is the right place for you. The shoes are made from wool, vinyl and other unusual materials and the colours will knock your socks off (quite literally!). Each design is exclusive and some bear evocative names, such as 'Moneywalker'.

Manolo Blahnik

31 W 54th Street
(between 5th and 6th
Ave., B2)
☎ 582 30 07
Subway 5th Ave.
Open every day 10.30am-
6.30pm.

The well-to-do and the world's most beautiful women come to find shoes to die for in this opulent and very, very expensive shop (the prices are not overtly displayed).

The top-quality shoes are original and innovative yet at the same time elegant.

Timberland

709 Madison Avenue
(at 62nd St., B1)
☎ 754 04 34
Subway 59th St.
Open Mon.-Fri. 9.30am-7pm,
Thu. until 8pm,
Sat. 10am-6pm, Sun. noon-6pm.

This shop is entirely devoted to casual shoes for men and women, with a wider choice of styles than elsewhere and, above all, prices are up to 50% lower. This is also

SAME SHOES, DIFFERENT SIZES

Remember, American shoe sizes are different to those back home. See the conversion tables on p. XV of the colour pages for more information on sizes in general.

Europe	36	37	38	39	40	41
US women's	5	6	7	8	9	10

your chance to discover the full range of practical Timberland clothes and accessories, which are of very good quality and able to withstand any weather.

LEATHER GOODS

Crouch & Fitzgerald

400 Madison Avenue
(at 48th St., B2)
☎ **755 58 88**
Subway 5th Ave.
Open Mon.-Sat. 9am-6pm.

Since 1839, Crouch & Fitzgerald have certainly lived up to their reputation as purveyors of the very finest leather goods, with top-quality ladies' handbags, briefcases, document wallets and men's belts made of beautifully finished

Hans Kock Ltd

174 Prince Street (B3)
☎ **226 53 85**
Subway Prince St.
Open Sun.-Thu. noon-8pm,
Fri.-Sat. noon-9pm, Sun.
1-8pm.

If you like fine leather, up-to-date styles, and colours other than grey, black or brown, then this is the place for you. Hans Kock is the darling of New Yorkers, who adore his slightly eccentric fashion accessories. The very trendy 1950s and streetwear-style bags (from $320) come in a dazzling range of colours, and pastel shades and the belts ($150) are all cleverly coordinated with the shop's highly original jewellery collection.

Coach

595 Madison
Avenue
(at 57th St., B1)
☎ **754 00 41**
Subway 5th Ave.
Open Mon.-Sat. 10am-8pm,
Sun. 11am-6pm.

The most famous leather goods shop and an institution in the United States. With an impressive choice of very fine leather articles (bags, belts, wallets and office accessories) in all the latest colours and in traditional or contemporary styles, you're sure to find something to please. High prices for high-quality goods, most of them guaranteed for life.

HATS

The Hat Shop

120 Thompson Street (B3)
☎ **219 14 45**
Subway Spring St.-6th Ave.
or Prince St.
Open Mon.-Sat. noon-7pm,
Sun. 1-6pm.

Handmade hats to make heads turn by a designer who has opened her own shop. Eye-catching designs to suit all tastes, including some very unusual ones – a range of taller and taller leather hats, berets, and pixie caps decorated with muslin, feathers, brooches and hatpins (from $20 to $600). If you like, you can also have a hat made to measure, a rare luxury that will be ready in just a few days.

leather or hide. All the best makes can be found here, including French (Louis Vuitton), Italian (Botega Veneta) and American (Cooney & Bourke) brands. As you may have expected, prices are astronomical, starting at $500 for the smallest leather pouch.

JEWELLERY

Stuart Moore

128 Prince Street (B3)
☎ 941 10 23
Subway Prince St.
Open Mon.-Sat. noon-
6.30pm, Sun. noon-5.30pm.

This jewellery shop sells original
contemporary pieces by European
designers (Swiss and German)
in a superb range of materials
and designs. With jewellery
for women and cuff links
and watches for men,
there's something for
everyone, and all at
very affordable
prices.

Tourneau Time Machine

**57th Street
(at Madison Ave., B2)**
☎ 758 73 00
Subway 59th St.
Open Mon.-Sat. 10am-6pm,
Thu. until 7pm, Sun.
11.30am-5.30pm.

Imagine a department store
entirely devoted to

watches – in
all, three floors of them –
with over 7,000
watches of
70 different
makes as
well as an
interesting
selection of old watches.

In addition to all this, several
exhibitions a year are held in the
small basement. If you can't find
a watch to suit you here, you're
unlikely to find it elsewhere.

GLASSES

Oliver Peoples

366 West Broadway (B3)
☎ 925 54 00
Subway Spring St.
Open Mon.-Sat. 11am-7pm,
Sun. noon-6pm.

Oliver Peoples, whose glasses are
currently all the rage in
America, opened his first New
York shop here, selling
attractive styles, both
retro and modern,
and a superb range
of sunglasses and
clips. Prices are
lower here than
in shops
outside the
United States.

Selima Optique

59 Wooster Street (B3)
☎ 343 94 90
Subway Spring St.
Open Mon.-Sat.
11am-7pm (Thu. to
8pm), Sun. noon-
7pm.

You'll find no
shy and retiring
librarians in this very trendy but
welcoming shop, with its wide
range of glasses and sunglasses.
The models designed by Selima
include 1970s-style creations as
well as the hippest

look for the 21st century.
You'll find Gucci and
Armani

frames, too. Keep an eye
out for the lovely hat
collection.

LINGERIE

Victoria's Secret

**34 E 57th Street
(at Madison Ave., B2)**
☎ 758 55 92
Subway 5th Ave.
Open Mon.-Sat. 10am-8pm,
Sun. noon-7pm.

A great place to buy high-quality
lingerie at affordable prices

The famous Victoria's Secret.

(around $30 for a bra). Sets in satin or floral cotton, gorgeous lace bodies and a mouth-watering range of negligées in trendy fabrics, such as patterned velvet. You'll also find perfume and a collection of tights to go with every outfit.

Elnera

485 E 7th Street (between 1st and 2nd Ave., B3)
☎ 473 24 54
Subway Astor Place or 2nd Ave.
Open Sun.-Wed. noon-8.30pm, Thu.-Fri. Noon-9.30pm, Sat. noon-9pm.

This small shop in the East Village has a wide range of lingerie that is both sexy and sophisticated, using lovely fabrics and tasteful motifs. Stock is not always plentiful, so if you see something you like, snap it up instantly. Some designs are quite expensive but you'll find some reasonably priced 100% silk models, too.

HANDBAGS

Kate Spade

454 Broome Street (on corner of Mercer St., B3)
☎ 274 19 91
www.katespade.com
Subway Prince St. or Spring St.
Open Mon.-Sat. 11am-5pm, Sun. noon-6pm.

Kate Spade's handbags are among the most keenly sought after bags in New York. They are always of excellent quality (watch out, a handbag can cost up to $300) and are classic in design. You can also buy sunglasses, diaries, wallets, pyjamas, picture frames and perfume before exploring her other shop – Kate Spade Travel – just four blocks away at 59 Thompson Street.

Manhattan Portage

333 E 9th Street (between 1st and 2nd Ave., B3)
☎ 995 54 90
www.manhattanportage.com
Subway Astor Place or 1st Avenue
Open Sun.-Tue. noon-7pm, Wed.-Sat. 10am-10pm.

This label was launched in 1980 and has been a great success, partly due to its hugely popular and highly practical 'Messenger Bags.' It specialises in hard-wearing, nylon bags in a wide range of colours alongside versatile and comfortable backpacks and other practical designs (from around $30). There's a bag for everyone (as their motto says).

MEN'S FASHION

New York is as renowned for its mens' clothes as for its ladies' and all the well-known designers show their collections here. Even men who really dislike shopping will be won over by the wide variety of styles on offer – from traditional classic and casual to sportswear and street fashion.

Moe Ginsburg
162 5th Avenue (B3)
☎ 242 34 82
Subway 23rd St.
Open Mon., Wed. & Fri.
10am-7pm, Thu. 10am-8pm,
Sat.-Sun. 11am-6pm.

It's not easy to find the entrance to this store, which is spread over no less than five floors. The door is in a very ordinary-looking building and there's a main lift that takes you to each of the levels. Inside the departments are relaxed and chic, with a wide choice of Italian clothes for Latin lovers and smart businessmen who want to stand out from the crowd.

Barneys
660 Madison Avenue (B1)
☎ 826 89 00
Subway 59th St.
Open Mon.-Fri. 10am-8pm,
Sat. 10am-7pm, Sun. 11am-6pm.

New York businessmen have adopted Barneys as their fashion mecca. All the latest designers are represented here and another outlet has opened in the heart of Chelsea (236 W 18th Street), at which the February and August sales offer all stock at 50-80% off. It's worth being in the know.

Brooks Brothers
346 Madison Avenue
(at E 44th St., B2)
☎ 682 88 00
www.brooksbrothers.com
Subway Grand Central
Open Mon.-Sat. 9am-7pm,
Thu. 9am-8pm, Sun.
noon-6pm.

Brooks Brothers, the traditional menswear shop, has dressed Presidents, film stars and celebrities. The suits are of excellent quality – very sober and elegant and made from the finest materials – and there's also a wide choice of ties, shirts, cuff links and eaux de cologne, as well as extremely comfortable underwear (at only $15), so you can dress yourself here from head to toe.

Kenneth Cole
610 5th Avenue (B2)
☎ 373 58 00
Subway Rockefeller Center
Open Mon.-Sun. 10am-8pm,
Sun. noon-7pm.

This American label is both classic and trendy in style, and is sported by men and women alike. The fabrics are always of excellent quality (in particular the leather) and the prices are quite reasonable (around $200 for a leather jacket). There's also a wide range of accessories including sunglasses, belts and shoes, the latter being particularly interesting.

Paul Smith

108 5th Avenue (between 15th and 16th St., B3), ☎ 627 97 70 Subway 14th St. or 6th Ave. Open Mon.-Wed., Fri. and Sat. 11am-7pm, Thu. 11am-8pm, Sun. noon-6pm.

Paul Smith sells a very British style of chic clothing for the gentleman who prefers a casual style. All the clothes, from shirts to two and three-piece suits, are a perfect blend of top-quality fabric and luxurious cut. You'll also find an extensive range of accessories here, including socks, scarves, ties, cuff links and matching umbrellas, for that total look.

Abercrombie & Fitch

199 Water Street (B4) ☎ 809 90 00 www.abercrombie.com Subway Fulton St. Open Mon.-Sat. 10am-7pm, Sun. 11am-6pm.

Behind the English name lies the favourite shop of American students. An easy-going, slightly yuppy, slightly sloppy look, with striped polo shirts and extra-wide canvas trousers. Ideal for the weekend or sport. The clothes are made from very tough fabrics and come in a wide variety of colours.

J. Crew

99 Prince Street (B3) ☎ 966 27 39 www.jcrew.com Subway Prince St. Open Mon., Wed., Fri. 10am-8pm, Tue., Thu., Sat. 10am-9pm, Sun. 11am-7pm.

This shop belonging to the mail order company of the same name offers both casual and fashionable clothes that are more sophisticated than GAP, with a wide choice of shirts and amusing underpants at reasonable prices. The look is rather 'preppy', with soft knit roll neck sweaters, khakis and corduroy trousers. The women's department is just as attractive, with a wonderful selection of swimwear every spring.

Banana Republic Men's

114 5th Avenue (between 16th and 17th St., B3) ☎ 366 46 30 Subway 14th St. or 6th Ave. Open Mon.-Fri. 10am-9pm, Sat. 10am-8pm, Sun. 11am-7pm.

This shop is a great one-stop spot for busy people who are looking for stylish, top quality menswear, including classic suits, shirts, jeans, pullovers or T-shirts. The prices are quite reasonable (you'll pay around $100 for a pair of smart trousers).

CALVIN KLEIN

654 Madison Avenue (at 60th St., B2) ☎ 292 90 00 Subway 59th St. Open Mon.-Wed., Fri.-Sat. 10am-6pm, Thu. 10am-7pm, Sun. noon-6pm.

This marvellous shop with high-ceilings and two floors of merchandise, is very simply decorated. The white walls, columns and odd glass table make a perfect backdrop for the elegant clothes and fine fabrics. This famous designer is now making a great impact on teenagers who are on the lookout for trendy, casual, yet elegant clothes. If you can't afford anything else, at least take home a pair of the famous underpants (around $12) with you (making sure you allow the label to show above the belt of your jeans!).

CHILDREN'S FASHION

With so many shops to choose from and such attractive prices, shopping in New York for the very young (and their older brothers and sisters) is a real pleasure. All the department stores have a large children's clothing department.

Old Navy belongs to the same company as Gap but its range of clothing is quite different in style, specializing in jeans and streetwear, with a collection of designs that are simple, comfortable and made from practical, hard-wearing fabrics – all perfect for active little babies and tots. Jeans cost around $20, dresses $16 and dungarees for tiny tots around $15.

and there are a great number of styles to choose from, including some fun ones. Boys' and girls' clothes from infants to age 12.

Greenstones
442 Columbus Avenue (at 81st St., A1)
☎ 580 43 22
Subway 81st St.
Open Mon.-Sat. 10am-7pm, Sun. noon-6pm.

All the world's brand names are represented here, including American, English, French and even Japanese. A very traditional shop, where you'll find chunky handmade pullovers in rich shades. More modern fabrics are used for the sporty outfits. For birthdays, they even have the ideal party hat, trimmed with satin and pompoms and sporting 'Happy Birthday' in glitter. Very difficult to resist in spite of the high prices, which are justified by the excellent quality.

Old Navy
503-511 Broadway (near Spring St., B3)
☎ 226 08 65
Subway Prince St. or Spring St.
Open Mon.-Sat. 9am-9pm, Sun. 10am-8pm.

Oshkosh B'Gosh
586 5th Avenue (at 48th St., B2)
☎ 827 00 98
Subway Rockefeller Center
Open Mon.-Fri. 10am-7pm, Sat. 10am-6pm, Sun. noon-5pm

The well-known children's dungarees are reasonably priced

Socks, T-shirts and sweaters to go with the dungarees (priced from only $10!) complete the outfits.

Space Kiddets
46 E 21st Street (between Broadway and Park Ave. South, B2)
☎ 420 98 78
Subway 23rd St.
Open Mon., Tue., Fri. 10.30am-6pm, Wed.-Thu. 10.30am-7pm, Sat. 10.30am-5.30pm.

A dream of a place where you'll find everything you need for your offspring, from toys and gadgets to feeding bottles and dummies, right in the middle of an eye-catching display of clothes for 0-13 years. Bootees and city shoes

t side by side with little cowboy
oots. And if you've run out of
deas for party outfits, you'll find
lenty of fancy dress clothes here.

Baby GAP

1037 Lexington Avenue
(at 74th St., B1)
☎ 327 26 14
Subway 77th St.
Open Mon.-Fri. 10am-8pm,
Sat. 10am-7.30pm, Sun.
11am-7pm.

Even if you're not a great fan of
the GAP adult range, you'll find
yourself charmed by their
collection for babies and toddlers.
The quality is excellent, the prices
are interesting (much lower than
in Europe), and there's a wide
choice of styles on offer. For
older children there's GAP Kids
(60 W 34th Street), which sells
clothes resembling those in the
adult stores.

Julian and Sara

103 Mercer Street (between
Spring and Prince St., B3)
☎ 226 19 89
Subway Prince St.
Open Mon.-Fri. 11am-7pm,
Sat.-Sun. 11.30am-6pm.

You'll recognise Julian and Sara's
by the penguin sign. Inside, the
shop is so small you wonder how
it can possibly hold so many
clothes, accessories and toys. The
pretty designs by American and
European dressmakers are all of
excellent quality, and this is an
address many New York mothers
keep a note of so that they can
dress their children in style.

Lilliput

265 Lafayette Street
(at Prince St., B3)
☎ 965 95 67
Subway Prince St. or
Spring St.
Open Mon.-Sat. 11am-7pm,
Sun. noon-6pm.

At last a shop selling trendy
clothes for the very young at
highly affordable prices. The
trend is towards streetwear and
futuristic fabrics. At Lilliput you'll
find a range of little suits in bright
orange or acid shades for $150,
sweaters from $49 and hats for
around $40. If the new items are
out of your price range, visit the
secondhand department – the
clothes are just as up to date and
much less expensive.

Magic Windows

1186 Madison Avenue
(between 86th and
87th St., B1)
☎ 289 00 28
Subway 86th St.
Open Mon.-Sat. 10am-6pm,
Sun. 11am-5pm.

If you want to dress your offspring
in smart, traditional clothes, you
owe it to yourself to pop along to
Magic Window. The regular
customers come here to buy
their school uniforms and
evening clothes.
The simplest
pullover costs
at least $100, but
you'll have three sales
assistants to serve
you. One of those
true luxury
shops that's

really worth a detour.
Naturally, you can be sure
of the quality, and the choice
is extensive.

THE EXCLUSIVE OILILY STORE

870 Madison Avenue
(between 70th and
71st St., B1)
☎ 628 01 00
Subway 68th St.
Open Mon.-Sat. 10am-6pm,
Sun. noon-5pm.

The beautiful clothes at
the Exclusive Oilily Store
are a play of colours and
patterns, and a real bouquet
of flowers awaits you as you
enter the shop. From baby
shoes to dungarees for older
children and Norwegian-style
pullovers, there's a riot of
colour throughout the shop.
With the prices sky high (from
$300 for a pullover), your
children will have to be very
good if they
want you to
buy them one
of these lovely
outfits.

SPORTSWEAR

I t's impossible to cross Manhattan without passing joggers, cyclists, teenagers on roller blades or basketball fans playing a few improvised games. The New Yorkers' unbridled passion for sport helps them combat stress and they long ago started the casual, sportswear look now all the rage around the world – jeans, trainers and polo shirts with big-name logos (Nike, Reebok, etc.).

JEANS

The Original Levi's Store

750 Lexington Avenue (at 59th St., B1)
☎ 826 59 57
Subway 59th St.
Open Mon.-Sat. 10am-8pm.

Levi's opened its first New York store here, not far from Bloomingdale's. Since then, the number of shops has never stopped growing. You can, of course, find here the entire collection of Levi's jeans, including the famous 501s (around $40), in an extensive range of colours.

SPORTS EQUIPMENT AND CLOTHES

Reebok Factory Direct Store

160 Columbus Avenue (at 67th St., A1)
Lincoln Center
☎ 595 14 80
Subway 66th St. or Lincoln Center
Open Mon.-Sat. 10am-8pm, Sun. noon-6pm.

If you want a new pair of sneakers or trainers this is *the* place to shop. Nike's great rival sells models which are just as hip but much better value ($50-100 for a pair of men's sneakers). Above the shop you'll find the famous Reebok gym, considered to be one of the biggest and best in Manhattan, complete with top of the range equipment, helpful staff, steam room, sauna and jacuzzi.

Blades Board and Skate

659 Broadway (between Bleecker and 3rd St., B3)
☎ 477 73 50
Subway Astor Place
Open Mon.-Sat. 11am-9pm, Sun. 11am-5pm.

It's hard to imagine anywhere with a more complete range of roller skates. This is everything a specialised shop should be, with a particularly well-stocked clothing and bag department for downhill addicts. Also a wide choice of skateboards and snowboards with original designs. Roller blades from $200.

Supreme

274 Lafayette Street (at Prince St., B3)
☎ 966 77 99
Subway Broadway-Lafayette
Open Mon.-Sat. 11.30am-7pm, Sun noon-6pm.

Skate fanatics congregate in front of this shop, so you can't miss it. It's here at Supreme that the latest in skateboards, fashion accessories, clothing, watches, stopwatches and trainers can be found. With

uch a wide range to choose from, he specialists still haven't ome up with any place to eat it.

Paragon Sporting Goods Company

867 Broadway
(at 18th St., B3)
☎ 255 80 36
Subway 14th St./Union Square
Open Mon.-Sat. 10am-8pm,
Sun. 11am-6.30pm.

It's difficult to talk about sports shops without mentioning a place that's become an institution. It stocks a wide range, but is falling behind the times due to competition from the smaller, more specialised shops. Even so, you'll find everything you need for sport in general here, with a good choice of swimwear, surfing gear (currently top of the fashion stakes) and walking boots.

Patagonia

101 Wooster Street
(between Prince St. and
Spring St., B3)
☎ 343 17 76
Subway Spring St.
Open Mon.-Sat. 11am- 7pm,
Sun. noon-6pm.

This shop is known for its sports clothes, and for mountaineering wear in

particular. Patagonia has developed a type of polyester that's as soft as lambswool and keeps you warm and cosy. The jackets and sweatshirts come in a range of very colourful styles.

SNEAKERS & TRAINERS

NikeTown

6 E 57th Street
(between 5th and
Madison Ave., B2)
☎ 891 64 53
Subway 5th Ave.
Open Mon.-Fri. 10am-8pm,
Sat. 10am-7pm,
Sun. 11am-6pm.

Gigantism Nike-style. Behind a façade masquerading as an old gym, five floors and 6,000m²/ 65,000sqft of space are devoted to the brand's products, with, of course, dozens of styles of shoes. Watch out – Nike's prices are on the up. Sneakers cost up to $140.

Foot Locker

734 Broadway (B3)
☎ 995 03 81
Subway 8th St.
Open Mon.-Sat. 10am-8pm,
Sun. 11am-6pm.

This shop isn't the only one of its kind – there are Foot Lockers on every street corner. And a good thing, too, since they sell one of the best selections of trainers. All the well-known brands and latest styles are available here at very reasonable prices.

NBA Store

666 5th Avenue (between
52nd and 53rd St., B2)
☎ 515 62 21
www.store.nba.com
Subway 5th Avenue
Open Mon.-Sat. 11am-7pm,
Sun. 11am-6pm.

NBA is not just a shop – it's a monument to basketball. Here you'll find all the equipment and merchandise associated with the

sport, including American team jerseys and a whole bunch of accessories, such as ball bags, towels, watches, socks and pens, all bearing your team's logo. Enjoy a spot of on location training, watch a match on the widescreen or have a coffee.

BEATY PRODUCTS

The subject of beauty has always been very close to the heart of appearance-conscious New Yorkers. In recent years the city has seen a huge increase in the number of stores selling plant-based products or those which contain natural ingredients. Essential oils and aromatherapy are very popular among the folk of New York, who use them to combat stress in the big city.

Aveda
**140 5th Avenue
(at 19th St., B3)
☎ 645 47 97
Subway 23rd St.
Open Mon.-Fri. 11am-8pm,
Sat. noon-7pm, Sun. noon-
6pm.**

Aveda has an exclusive collection of body, skin and hair care products together with a range of make-up, all made with natural plant, herb and flower extracts. If you're in the mood for a spot of pampering, try some of the wonderful oils. The store also offers a range of beauty treatments.

Kiehl's
**109 3rd Avenue
(at 13th St., B3)
☎ 677 31 71
www.kiehls.com
Subway 14th St.-Union Sq.
Open Mon.-Fri. 10am-
6.30pm (Thu. to 7.30pm),
Sat. 10am-6pm, Sun. noon-
6pm.**

Khiel's has been around since 1851 and is an institution for New Yorkers, its walls oozing tradition. Their lip balm is famous and their body lotions are very popular. Everything here is excellent quality – you won't be disappointed.

Face Stockholm
**110 Prince Street (between
Wooster and Greene St., B3)
☎ 966 91 10
Subway Prince St.
Open Mon.-Wed. 11am-7pm,
Thu.-Sat. 11am-8pm, Sun.
noon-6pm.**

This store, with its simple yet effective decor, offers a wide selection of professional make-up products, including lipsticks (around $14), eye pencils ($7). They provide free sponges and excellent advice if you're thinking of a complete make-over. Try the wonderful range of liquid foundations which come in 10 different shades.

Boyds Madison Avenue
**655 Madison Avenue (between
60th and 61st St., B2)
☎ 838 65 58
www.boydsnyc.com
Subway 59th St.
Open Mon.-Fri. 8.30am-
7.30pm, Sat. 9.30am-7pm,
Sun. noon-6pm.**

Don't be overwhelmed by the somewhat ostentatious window display – Boyd's is a great department store as well as a pharmacy, with its own very popular cosmetic range (Renoir), used by such celebrities as Cher, Lauren Bacall and Meryl Streep. The store opened 50 years ago and boasts one of the most complete ranges of well-known cosmetics and hair and nail accessories.

MAC

**413 Spring Street (between
Greene and Mercer St., B3)
☎ 334 46 41
www.maccosmetics.com
Subway Spring St. or
Prince St.
Open Mon.-Sat. 11am-
7pm, Sun. noon-6pm.**

MAC (Make-up Art
Cosmetics) was launched
in 1984 by two
Canadian
professional
make-up artists,
Frank Angelo and
Frank Toskan, and has become a
huge international success, mostly
due to the incredible popularity
of their eye shadows and lipsticks,
which are available in every
possible colour and tone (their
frosted range alone comes in 49
different shades!). Lipsticks cost
$14 and eye shadows between
$12.50 and $14. MAC fans will be
in paradise.

Helena Rubinstein

**135 Spring Street (between
Wooster and Greene St., B3)
☎ 343 99 63
Subway Spring St.
or Prince St.
Open Mon. 11am-7pm,
Tue.-Fri. 11am-8pm,
Sat. 10am-6pm, Sun. noon-
6pm.**

Helena Rubenstein is a haven of
peace in busy SoHo, where you
can try the complete range of
beauty products and make-up at
your leisure. Their 'Illumination'
foundation compact is available
in 10 lovely colours. Behind the
thick red velvet curtains you'll find
a fabulous beauty salon in which
you can be pampered like a
princess. While you wait between
treatments, you can sit back and
relax and enjoy a little cake or two,
courtesy of the salon.

Elizabeth Arden

**691 5th Avenue
(at 54th St., B2)
☎ 546 02 00
Subway 5th Avenue
Open Mon.-Wed. 10am-
7pm, Thu.-Fri. 10am-9pm,
Sat. 10am-8pm, Sun.
11am-6pm.**

A doorman in a smart livery
awaits to open the doors of this
store for you. What the place lacks
in atmosphere, it more than
makes up for with its wonderful
range of high quality products.
The 'Green Tea' range is certainly
worth a try – the delicately-
perfumed body lotion and the
calming body balm are a real

pleasure. At the back
of the shop is the
Red Door Salon,
where a whole

programme of
beauty treatments is on offer. A
massage will cost $90, a makeover
$55 and a manicure $35.

Davies Gate
and Philosophy

**Sephora
555 Broadway (between
Spring and Prince St., B3)
☎ 625 13 09
Subway Prince St.
Open Mon.-Wed. 10am-8pm,
Thu.-Sat. 10am-8.30pm,
Sun. 11am-7pm.**

Davies Gate and Philosophy are
both American companies that
make beauty products exclusively

FRESH

**57 Spring Street
(between Lafayette
and Mulberry St., B3)
☎ 925 00 99
Subway Spring St.
Open Mon.-Sat. 10am-
8pm, Sun. noon-6pm.**

Fresh is an American brand,
originating in Boston, which
has become extremely popular
with New Yorkers. Their concept
is to combine ancient beauty
rituals and natural remedies
with cutting edge technology to
produce a range of beauty
products made from natural
ingredients, such as sugar,
milk, honey or soya. The 'Milk'
body lotion, the 'Soy' face
cream and the 'Umbrian Clay'
treatment bar are just a few of
the wonderful choices on offer.
The atmosphere is warm and
welcoming and you're bound to
come out with something that
takes your fancy.

from natural products. The texture
of their skin care range is creamy,
the scent lovely and the packaging
a delight. David Gate's Whole
Wheat Body Lotion is sublime
and the jojoba hand cream
incredibly soothing. Philosophy
lets its collection speak for itself
(literally) with its products such
as 'Change Me', 'Be Somebody'
and 'Message in a Bottle'
conveying their message loud
and clear. It's easy to see why
'Hope in a Jar' is such a big seller.

INTERIOR DESIGN

New Yorkers attach enormous importance to interior design and the shops selling goods for the home in the city reflect this interest, with wonderful items on offer, such as household linens (with top-quality cotton articles at unbeatable prices), tableware and lamps, all available in the very latest styles. You're sure to find something to add that special finishing touch to your home.

Fishs Eddy

889 Broadway
(at 19th St., B3)
☎ 420 90 20
Subway Union Square
Open Mon.-Sat. 10am-9pm,
Sun. 11am-7pm.

With its old New England farm decor, Fishs Eddy has a country atmosphere in the heart of Manhattan. Background music from the 1940s and 1950s plays while you browse among the piles of plates – the store specialises in buying up tableware from hotels, clubs and colleges that have closed down. There are some exclusive designs as well as some very amusing ones, and stock changes constantly. Pieces with old-fashioned designs will give an original touch to your table, and prices start at just $1.50 for a plate.

Williams-Sonoma

1175 Madison Avenue
(at 86th St., B2)
☎ 289 68 32
Subway 86th St.
Open Mon.-Fri. 10am-7pm,
Sat. 10am-6pm, Sun. noon-6pm.

Started by the same firm as Pottery Barn, Williams-Sonoma specialises in everything remotely connected with cooking and the art of entertaining (utensils, decorative tableware, household linen, etc.). Good food lovers will find everything they could possibly need here to prepare and present their favourite dishes to perfection

Bed, Bath & Beyond

620 6th Avenue
(at 18th St., B3)
☎ 255 35 50
Subway 14th St.
Open Mon.-Sun. 9am-9pm.

This is a one-stop shopping experience for those wanting household items such as bedlinen, towels, blankets, picture frames – you name it, they've got it. The prices are good and the quality excellent. Shopping baskets to the ready!

Pottery Barn

600 Broadway
(at Houston St., B2)
☎ 219 24 20
Subway Broadway-Lafayette
Open Mon.-Sat. 10am-9pm,
Sun. 11am-7pm.

Pottery Barn faces stiff competition from Crate & Barrel, stocking a very similar range of

products – a selection of modern kitchen utensils and household objects (cups, bowls, dishes, glasses and cutlery) at very acceptable prices (generally $10-20 per item). You'll also find decorative objects for your home, such as mirrors, candlesticks, dried flowers and lamps.

Broadway Panhandler

**477 Broome Street
(at Wooster St., B3)
☎ 966 34 34
Subway Spring St.
Open Mon.-Fri. 10.30am-7pm, Sat. 11am-7pm, Sun. 11am-6pm.**

Everything you could possibly need for the kitchen

can be found in Broadway Panhandler, from the smallest and most basic of items to top of the range gadgets and equipment. If you're looking for an authentic Chinese wok or an Italian cappuccino machine, you're in the right place. The range of cake decorations is quite exquisite.

Simon Pearce

**120 Wooster Street
(at Prince St., B3)
☎ 334 23 93
Subway Prince St.
Open Mon.-Sat. 11am-7pm, Sun. noon-6pm.**

Very beautiful household objects, grey-green tableware, glassware and lovely, simple wooden articles

(dishes and chopping boards). An ideal place to choose for your wedding list – though perhaps a little far from home!

Mood Indigo

**181 Prince Street
(at Sullivan St., B3)
☎ 254 11 76
Subway Prince St.
Open Tue.-Sat. noon-7pm, Sun. 1-6pm.**

This little shop is the ideal place for fans of Art Deco tableware and kitchen utensils, with cutlery sets, chrome dishes, salt cellars and pepper pots in unusual shapes. A very fine collection of objects though perhaps a little pricey – expect to pay around $28 for a coffee cup and $42 for a large dish.

Crate & Barrel

**650 Madison Avenue
(at 59th St., B2)
☎ 308 00 11
Subway 59th St.
Open Mon.-Fri. 10am-8pm, Sat. 10am-7pm, Sun. noon-6pm.**

In this wood-panelled shop, you'll find a selection of fine wooden and ceramic objects, household linen, crockery and kitchen utensils. The accent is on neutral tones and traditional materials, which gives the merchandise a fresh, natural look. The prices are very reasonable, with many articles costing under $25. The style lies somewhere between IKEA and Habitat – Crate & Barrel is like a GAP for the home.

atmosphere and a vast selection of bath products (try the tea-based ones), thick towels, shower curtains and bath mats. There's also a lovely collection of multi-coloured straw and fine fabric boxes and some adorable teddy bears. A wide range of prices means everyone will find something to suit them.

Leekan Designs

93 Mercer Street
(at Spring St., B3)
☎ 226 72 26
Subway Prince St.
Open Mon.-Fri. 11am-6pm,
Sat. 11am-7pm, Sun. noon-6pm.

Specialising in decorative objects from Asia, this shop is well worth a visit. It's a real treasure trove, where you'll find a selection of jewellery, loose turquoise stones for $2 (to make your own bracelets, earrings, etc.), beads, tribal masks (from $150), batik fabric and a collection of variously-sized Japanese scissors.

The Apartment

101 Crosby Street (B3)
☎ 219 36 61
Subway Prince St.
or Spring St.
Open Mon.-Sat. 11am-7pm,
Sun. noon-6pm.

Stéphane Boubli and Gina Alvarez have come up with the original idea of creating a furniture and interiors shop situated in an actual apartment. Everything is for sale in this loft space, from the furniture to the smallest picture frame. The atmosphere is very welcoming and pleasant and you can see everything in its proper setting.
You'll be offered a coffee and you won't be bothered by the sales assistants if you fancy sitting down for a while to chat to friends. The products are trendy and modern but the prices high (around $100 for a little fake-fur cushion).

Ad*Hoc

136 Wooster Street (between
Prince and Houston St., B3)
☎ 748 48 52
Subway Lexington Ave.
Open Mon.-Thu. 11am-7pm,
Fri. & Sat. 11am-8pm,
Sun. 11am-6pm.

This shop selling household and bathroom accessories has a very sophisticated loft

Terra Verde

120 Wooster Street
(at Prince St., B3)
☎ 925 45 33
Subway Prince St.
Open Mon.-Sat. 11am-7pm,
Sun. noon-6pm.

This is a mecca for furniture, linens, accessories and environmentally-friendly decorative objects, a unique place combining the decorative arts

with green issues. Architect William McDonough has entirely renovated the original shop space using non-toxic materials. You'll find an amazing range of household linen, such as cotton king-size duvet covers ($100), ideal for those with chemical allergies, as well as wooden toothbrushes, a variety of scented candles (honey, amber, etc.) and some marvellous candle holders, untreated wooden furniture and soap with unusual perfumes from $8.

Laytner's Linen & Home

**2270 Broadway
(at 82nd St.)
☎ 724 01 80
Subway 79th St.
Open Mon.-Fri.
10am-7.30pm, Sat. 10am-
6.30pm, Sun. noon-6pm.**

This is where to come for classic, stylish and tasteful items for the home. Everything is of excellent quality and there's a wide range of bedcovers and towels in all the colours you could wish for. The bathroom accessories are particularly attractive, with the shower curtains among some of the most original items.

Lechters Housewares

**10 W 34th Street (between
5th and 6th St., B3)
☎ 564 32 26
Subway 34th St.-Herald
Square
Open Mon.-Sat. 8am-9pm,
Sun. 10am-6pm.**

Just about everything for the kitchen (and some things for the bathroom, too) in this reasonably-priced chain of shops.

There's a wide choice of attractive picnic cutlery, glasses and plates, graters, wooden spoons and even mushroom, potato and maize brushes. Whether absolutely necessary, they're always practical and definitely what you or your friends have been looking for.

Artemide

**46 Greene Street (B3)
☎ 925 15 88
Subway Prince St.
Open Mon.-Fri. 10am-5pm,
Sat. 11am-6pm.**

This gallery-shop is entirely dedicated to lamps made by a team of designers working in close partnership. The lamps are all quite striking and original, with simple, futuristic shapes retaining just a few traditional touches. Very beautiful objects with prices ranging from $200-1,000.

Kar'ikter

**19 Prince Street
☎ 274 19 66
Subway Prince St.
Open Mon.-Sun.
11am-7.30pm.**

You're sure to love this little shop, set in the heart of NoLiTa. Kar'ikter specialises in contemporary European products, and the

PORTICO BED & BATH

**72 Spring Street (B3)
☎ 941 78 00
Subway Spring St.
Open Mon.-Sat. 11am-7pm
(Thu. to 8pm),
Sun. noon-6pm.**

A very attractive selection of articles for the home, including household linen, sheets, bathroom accessories (sponges, brushes, shaving brushes, etc.), as well as a range of environmentally-friendly body care products. Excellent quality untreated natural materials (cotton and linen), in pastel shades of beige, off-white, baby blue, etc., plain or striped. A few traditional cast-iron beds and some very fine furniture.

creations of many different designers are on display, not least those of the Italian design giant, Alessi. They also sell licensed European character books and merchandise, such as Tintin, Babar and Wallace and Gromit. It's a great place for presents.

MUSEUM SHOPS

You'll probably never have time to see all the collections housed in New York's wealth of museums, let alone its museum shops, where you'll find art books, reproductions, posters, postcards and other items bearing images of the great masters and masterpieces. However, they do sell original, high-quality products, that make excellent gifts or souvenirs. Some shops offer a shipping service, which allows you to avoid costly excess baggage charges.

The Metropolitan Museum of Art Shop

113 Prince Street (B3)
☎ 614 30 00
www.metmuseum.org
Subway Prince St.
Open Mon.-Fri. 11am-7.30pm, Sat., Sun. 10am-8pm.

This art bookshop attracts a discerning crowd of customers, as it's here you'll find the finest reproductions of great works of art and an impressive array of products at very reasonable prices. If you're fond of postcards, you can stock up on them here. Children will also find something to please them, with toys and objects based on items from the collection. As well as the shop at the museum itself, the Met has several other outlets in New York, including one in Macy's and at the airport.

Guggenheim Museum Store

1071 5th Avenue
(at 89th St., B1)
☎ 423 36 15
www.guggenheim.org
Subway 86th St.

Open Sun.-Wed. 9.30am-6.30pm, Thu. 10am-6pm, Fri.-Sat. 9.30am-8.30pm.

The shop, in the annexe of the Solomon R. Guggenheim Museum of modern painting, offers a wide choice of stationery (address books, writing paper, pens etc.), with reproductions of works of art from the collection. Posters and T-shirts based on the works of Kandinsky, Pollock and Klimt are difficult, if not impossible, to find elsewhere. It has a great many decorative objects and, of course, a good selection of art books.

The Museum of Modern Art Shop

Bookstore:
45-20 33rd Street, Queens
(at Queens Blvd, off map)
☎ 708 97 00
www.moma.org
Subway 33rd St.
Open Sat.-Thu. 10am-7pm, Fri. 10am-9pm.

The bookstore, temporarily relocated to the Queens location while MoMA undergoes its huge rebuilding project, sells a fine selection of books, postcards (50

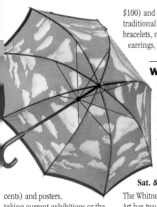

$100) and a superb collection of traditional silver jewellery – bracelets, necklaces, rings, earrings, hair jewellery, etc.

Whitney Museum Store

945 Madison Avenue (B1)
☎ 570 36 14
www.whitney.org
Subway 77th St.
Tue.-Thu. 11am-6pm, Fri. 1-9pm, Sat. & Sun. 11am-6pm.

The Whitney Museum of American Art has two shops, one in the museum itself and one in the basement. They stack a fine collection of contemporary art objects, often related to the exhibitions at the museum, and amusing and creative gift ideas at affordable prices, such as metal tableware in weird and wonderful shapes and plexiglass or hologram-effect jewellery.

cents) and posters, taking current exhibitions or the artists on show at the museum as their theme.

MoMA Design Store

81 Spring Street (B3)
☎ (646) 613 13 67
Subway Spring St.
Open Mon.-Sat. 11am-7pm, Sun. 11am-6pm.

Don't miss the MoMA Design Store, where you'll find superb reproductions of contemporary objects, such as vases, plates, jewellery and lamps, as well as an interesting range of environmentally-friendly products and original gadgets.

The Museum for African Art Shop

593 Broadway (B3)
☎ 966 13 13
Subway Prince St.
Open Tue.-Fri. 10.30am-5.30pm, Sat. & Sun. noon-6pm.

Handily located in the museum entrance, the shop sells very fine African artefacts – musical instruments, beautiful handmade fabrics (very expensive at around

The American Museum of Natural History Shop

Central Park West (between 79th and 81st St., A1)
☎ 769 51 00
Subway 81st St.
Open every day 10am-5.45pm (Sat. to 8.45pm).

The American Museum of Natural History's shop is where children will find the most fascinating and instructive objects – miniature reproductions of dinosaurs and wooden toys with a natural history slant, as well as a wide selection of minerals, fossils and shells. Schools will also find plenty to keep them happy among the many recycled products (T-shirts, bags, different kinds of paper, etc.).

THE AMERICAN FOLK ART MUSEUM SHOP

45 W 53rd Street (B2)
☎ 265 10 40
www.folkartmuseum.org
Subway 5th Ave.-53rd St.
Open every day 10am-6pm, (Fri. to 8pm).

The ideal place to find T-shirts, jewellery, decorative objects for the home and wooden toys decorated with traditional American patterns. Many of the products are handmade, including the marvellous patchwork quilts. There's also a shop at the museum annexe at 2 Lincoln Square (☎ 595 95 33, open every day 11am-7.30pm (Mon. to 6pm).

The Cooper Shop at the Jewish Museum

1109 5th Avenue (at 92nd St., B1)
☎ 423 32 11
Subway 96th St.
Open Sun.-Mon., Wed.-Thu., 11am-5.45pm, Tue. 11am-8pm, Fri. 11am-3pm.

With its selection of stationery, books, CDs, videos and jewellery, this shop in the annexe of the Jewish Museum will fascinate anyone interested in Judaism. There's also another shop on the same site, called Celebrations (☎ 423 32 60), which sells finely crafted ceremonial objects, which are designed to commemorate Jewish holidays.

GADGETS AND CURIOSITIES

You've been warned – New York won't give you any respite, especially if you're keen on new gadgets. Every street, even the most ordinary, seems to have at least one specialised shop packed with customers anxious to see the latest novelties. Have a look round them yourself and see what the designers have come up with.

CHILDREN'S TOYS

FAO Schwarz

**767 5th Avenue
(at 58th St., B2)
☎ 644 94 00
Subway 5th Ave.
or Lexington Ave.
Open Mon.-Wed. 10am-6pm,
Thu.-Sat. 10am-7pm, Sun.
11am-6pm.**

The best-known toy shop, some would say the best – in other words an institution which has been open since 1862. The choice is quite unbelievable and beyond the wildest dreams of even the most imaginative of children. With animals, dolls, trains, cars, board games, etc., it's a magical place – fairyland in the heart of New York. The new baby section is really lovely.

Enchanted Forest

**85 Mercer Street (B3)
☎ 925 66 77
Subway Prince St.
Open Mon.-Sat. 11am-7pm,
Sun. noon-6pm.**

Books, handmade wooden toys, models, soft toys and piles of bric-a-brac for children (and grown-ups too!), all based around the theme of animals, nature and legends. It's a magical place, decorated with branches and greenery, which fires the imagination in children and evokes a sense of nostalgia in their parents. As you wander through the menagerie of beasts, you could be forgiven for thinking you really were in the depths of an enchanted forest.

Toys 'R' Us

**1514 Broadway (between
44th and 45 St., A2)
☎ 1 800 869 77 87
Subway Times Square-
42nd St.
Open Mon.-Fri. 10am-
9pm, Sat. & Sun.
11am-8pm.**

This huge chain of toyshops now has numerous branches outside the US, but nothing can really compare with a visit to the vast New York flagship store, which opened its doors in November 2001, right in the heart of Times

Square. Two of the many highlights include a life-size Barbie Doll house and a huge Jurassic Park dinosaur that roars as you approach it. It's a real treat for kids and fun for adults, too.

Tiny Doll House

1179 Lexington Avenue (at 80th St., B1)
☎ 744 37 19
Subway 77th St.
Open Mon.-Fri. 11am-5.30pm Sat. 11am-5pm

Absolutely everything in this wonderful shop is small-scale or minute. It specialises in doll houses, and all the accessories

that accompany them. There's a wide range of furniture, from tiny beds and chests for the bedroom, sofas and chairs for the living room to tennis racquets, books and potted plants, as well as the tiny dolls themselves. A veritable mecca for people who own dolls-houses of course, but also fascinating for those who just like marvelling at things in miniature.

Chimera

77 Mercer St (B3)
☎ 334 47 30
Subway Spring St.
Open Mon.-Sun. 11.30am-6pm (Sat. to 7pm).

Chimera, located in the heart of SoHo, sells a range of tasteful toys and gadgets that will capture the imagination of kids and adults alike. Animals come in all shapes and fabrics and the finger

puppets are adorable. There's also a large selection of books for children, both educational and entertaining.

GADGETS, CURIOSITIES AND SPECIALIST SHOPS

The Sharper Image

4 W 57th Street (A2)
☎ 265 25 50
Subway 5th Ave.
Open Mon.-Fri. 10am-7pm, Sat. 10am-6pm, Sun. noon-6pm.

Lots of more or less crazy gadgets you probably never thought you needed – such as a portable mini refrigerator that you can take to the office to keep your sandwiches fresh ($99.95), or a heated electric pocket massager ($99.95). The shop also sells all

kinds of more practical items, including luggage, binoculars, watches and hi-tech scales. Definately a place for people who have everything!

Big City Kite Company

1210 Lexington Avenue (at 82nd St., B1)
☎ 472 26 23
Open Mon., Tue. and Fri. 11am-6.30pm, Thu. 11am-7.30pm, Sat. 10am-6pm.

Kites are back in fashion. Come along and see for yourself in this inviting shop, which has over 150 different models on offer. You can hire a kite for a few hours, but not everyone is necessarily good at handling them so you can, if you like, have lessons at Big City Kite Company.

Evolution

120 Spring Street (B3)
☎ 343 11 14
Subway Spring St.
Open Sun.-Wed. 11am-7pm, Thu.-Sat. 11am-10pm.

The hanging skeleton that greets you as you cross the threshold of this shop sets the tone straight away – this nature store is full of surprises, many of which will bring you out in goose pimples. Among the traditional stuffed animals (such as a boa constrictor or mouse for $70), there's a whole collection of skulls, bones and even entire human skeletons.

KIDDING AROUND

60 W 15th Street (A3)
☎ 645 63 37
Subway 14th St.
or 6th Ave.
Open Mon.-Sat. 10am-
7pm, Sun. 11am-6pm.

In a market increasingly dominated by global chains, Kidding Around represents a dying breed – a charming, independently owned toy store. It's a real gold mine, full of toys (for 0 to 12 years), fancy dress costumes, tricks, games and gadgets. There are early development toys for babies and kits and models to inspire creativity and independent thinking. Little girls will adore the dressing-up area with its glittering tiaras and hair accessories, and there are loads of small pocket-money toys. There are some lovely hand knitted hats for around $30.

They even sell a range of giant insects in glass cases to hang on your wall, and, for your children,

lollies containing worms or insects. Their rather unusual sweets ($2) include honeyed or cheesy worms, which the little monsters are bound to enjoy.

Hotel Venus

382 West Broadway (B3)
☎ 966 40 66
Subway Spring St.-
6th Avenue
Open Mon.-Sun. 11am-8pm
(Sat. to 9pm).

Enter the strange new world of Hotel Venus, a bizarre basement store brimming with audacious accessories, gorgeous gadgets, hip household items, kitsch kitchen equipment and even a few cool clothes. The little notebooks covered in pink or orange fake fur are just irresistible. It's quite an experience, and it's the ideal place to pick up the 'odd' gift or two!

Sam Ash Music

155, 159, 160 and 163
W 48th Street (A2)
☎ 719 22 99
Subway 49th St.
Open Mon.-Fri. 11am-8pm,
Sat. 10am-7pm.

This chain of shops has been specialising in musical instruments for 76 years. There are four stores, selling new and secondhand instruments, as well as accessories, sound equipment, turntables, mixing desks and sheet music. They claim the prices of synthesizers are the lowest in the country, so it's certainly worth taking a look while you're here.

Tender Buttons

143 East 62nd Street (B2)
☎ 758 70 04
Subway Lexington Ave.
or 59th St.
Open Mon.-Fri. 11am-
6pm, Sat. 11am-5pm.

If you've lost a button off your favourite Renaissance-style waistcoat, you're bound to find one to replace it here. Tender Buttons only sells buttons and has an impressive number in stock, from enamel and carved bone to Indian silver

and Aboriginal wooden ones, including George Washington's jacket buttons (for $1,000). Unique designs, which are also sold as earrings and cuff links. Prices range from 50 cents to hundreds of dollars.

Rita Ford
Music Boxes

19 E 65th Street (between Madison and 5th Ave., B1)
☎ **379 66 36**
Subway Lexington Ave. or 68th St.
Open Mon.-Fri. Sat. 10am-9pm, Sat. 10am-7pm, Sun. noon-4pm.

Rita Ford transports us to the magical and enchanting world of musical boxes – not only the ones with the famous revolving ballerinas but also the old musical boxes of our grandmothers, some of which date back to the 19th century, as well as far more up-to-date versions based on Walt Disney characters (such as *Beauty and the Beast*). These rare pieces, some

Specialist collectors will direct you to this store, which overflows with American comic books. The traditional Batman and Spiderman are still around in both the original and updated versions, alongside the new cyber heroes and Japanese Mangas. There's also a wide range of figurines which you can paint yourself, together with videos and T-shirts sporting your favourite comic book hero.

of which are collector's items, are worth a small fortune, but the price seems entirely justified when you see the fine gold and silver work involved.

COMICS
AND FIGURINES

Village Comics

214 Sullivan Street (between Bleecker and W 3rd St.)
☎ **777 27 70**
Subway W 4th St.
Open Mon.-Tue. 10.30am-7.30pm, Wed.-Sat. 10.30am-8.30pm, Sun. 11am-7pm.

Love Saves the Day

119 2nd Avenue (at 7th St., B3)
☎ **228 38 02**
Subway Astor Place
Open Mon.-Sat. noon-8.30pm, Sun. noon-8pm.

A kitsch paradise, with old toys, figurines and memorabilia of comic book heroes and well-known stars. The stock includes vintage and repro items, including statuettes, magazines, dolls, pink neon lamps, clothing, as well as tawdry little tapestry Madonnas and virtually anything with Elvis on it. Elvis fans will be amazed… or appalled.

HI-FI AND COMPUTERS

New York is a dream of a place to buy electronic equipment, whether personal CD players, digital cameras or computers. There's no lack of choice and all the best makes can be found at very attractive prices. However, it's a good idea to do some research on how much similar items cost at home. Beware of problems relating to voltage conversion, adaptors, guarantees and customs, if you're taking goods out of the country (see p. 81).

The Wiz

726 Broadway
(at 7th St., B3)
☎ 677 41 11
Subway Astor Place
Open Mon.-Fri. 10am-9.30pm, Sat. 9am-9.30pm, Sun. 11-7pm.

This chain of shops prides itself on matching or beating the prices of any other electronics shop. There's a wide choice of hi-fi equipment and gadgets and regular special offers are advertised in the papers.

J&R Music & Computer World

23 Park Row
(near Beeckman St., B4)
☎ 238 90 00
Subway City Hall or Chambers St.
Open Mon.-Sat. 9am-6.30pm, Sun. 11am-6pm.

Behind City Hall lies this treasure trove of hi-fi and audio/video

equipment, together with discmans and digital cameras, all at bargain prices. Outstanding special offers take place every week (see the advertising page in the *Village Voice*). The music selection (classical, jazz, rock, etc.) is also very interesting. Next door is another store with five floors specialising in information technology. An entire floor is taken up by Apple products.

CompUSA

1775 Broadway
(at 57th St., A2)
☎ 262 97 11
Open Mon.-Fri. 9am-8pm, Sat. 10am-7pm, Sun. 11am-6pm.

This is as close as you'll get to a computer superstore in the city. CompUSA is an immense chain specializing in Macs and PCs.

There's a huge choice of models, including laptops, monitors, scanners and printers. Fans of computer games are certainly in the right place.

Uncle Steve

343 Canal Street (B4)
☎ 925 51 85
Subway Canal St.
Open every day 10am-7pm.

Uncle Steve is as popular as the Canal Street district in which it's located. You'll find a little of everything here, from fax machines and cameras to domestic robots. The prices are particularly competitive for stereo equipment (complete mini-systems from $200), video recorders, radios and televisions.

Grand Central Camera & Computer

**420 Lexington Avenue
(at 42nd St., B2)
☎ 986 22 70
Subway Grand Central-
Lexington Ave.
Open Mon.-Fri. 9am-8pm,
Sat. 9am-7pm,
Sun. 10am-6.30pm.**

At Grand Central Camera & Computer, you'll find a very wide choice of computers, cameras, camcorders and audio and video equipment, compatible with all standards. With everything at discount prices, it's well worth going along to take a look.

Ken Hansen

**509 Madison Ave. (between
52nd and 53rd St., B2)
☎ 317 09 23
Subway 5th Ave.
Open Mon.-Fri. 9am-5pm.**

This is one of the best places to buy professional photographic

equipment – all the well-known photographers shop here. Enjoy a choice of very high quality camera lenses and bodies plus accessories at relatively competitive prices. You'll also find secondhand equipment that's been very thoroughly overhauled.

B&H Photo

**420 9th Avenue (between
33rd and 34th St.)
☎ 444 50 40
Subway 34th St.-
Penn Station
Open Mon.-Thu. 9am-7pm,
Fri. 9am-2pm, Sun. 10am-
5pm.**

B&H is popular with New York professionals. It has every piece of photographic, sound or video equipment you could want. The prices are higher than at J&R, but there's a far greater choice.

Do phone ahead to check opening times, as the store closes on Jewish holidays and Saturdays, and you'll need to be patient – you may have to wait a while before being served. It's worth a visit.

BUYING ELECTRONIC GOODS

One of the best areas to shop for electronic goods is between 14th and 23rd Streets, and between Broadway and 6th Avenue. Here you'll find many stores specialising in cameras, computers, audio and video equipment, and so on. Turnover in these shops is fairly rapid, which in turn enables them to keep the prices relatively low, though its best to have an idea of the prices in other stores, or at home, so that you can do some careful comparisons. Remember that you may also have to pay customs duty (see p. 81), which will affect the cost of your 'bargain'. Don't forget to check compatibility with your own equipment before buying, and be aware that the US uses a different TV and video system from that in Europe, as well as a lower voltage, so you'll need to buy an adaptor (see p. 81).

MUSIC STORES

There are shops selling CDs and records absolutely everywhere in New York. Some small stores don't survive long against competition from the big chains, which regularly slash prices. Others manage to hold out by specialising in a particular style of music or selling collector's items. The prices are disconcertingly low and the choice is quite amazing. Have your credit cards handy!

CLASSICAL MUSIC

All the big chains have a classical music department. HMV's is very well stocked and the sales assistants are highly competent. You can take your time choosing as you listen to the latest releases.

Academy Record and CDs

12 W 18th Street (between 5th and 6th Ave., A3)
☎ 242 30 00
Subway 18th St.
Open Mon.-Sat. 9.30am-9pm, Sun 11am-7pm.

Classical music and opera have pride of place in this shop, located in the heart of Chelsea. The store has a large number of vinyl records as well as CDs on offer, which will delight purists. You'll also find a fine selection of old editions of books and a few music scores in this haven of peace. Their other branch, Academy LPs (77 E 10th Street, ☎ 780 91 66, open Mon.-Thu. noon-8pm, Fri. & Sat. noon-9pm, Sun. noon-6pm), sells jazz, pop and genre LPs.

JAZZ

Jazz Record Center

236 W 26th Street (between 7th and 8th Ave., A3)
8th floor
☎ 675 44 80
Subway 23rd St.
Open Mon.-Sat. 10am-6pm.

This is the best shop in New York for jazz music, not only for current works but also for old albums and the finest recordings by the great masters. The catalogue is quite exceptional and despatch can be arranged anywhere in the world.

Bleecker Street Records

239 Bleecker St. (A3)
☎ 255 78 99
Subway Christopher St.
Open Sun.-Thu. 11am-10pm, Fri.-Sat. 11-1am.

For fans of vintage recordings this is one of the most highly-specialised record stores in the Village, in particular for jazz but also for blues and gospel. It has an impressive quantity of vinyl records, especially 45s, rare albums and collector's items.

HIP-HOP, DANCE AND TECHNO

Fat Beats

**406 6th Avenue
(between 8th and 9th St., B3)
☎ 673 38 83
Subway W 4th St.
Open Sun. noon-8pm,
Mon.-Thu. noon-9pm,
Fri. -Sat. noon-10pm.**

A tiny shop where you'll find the latest hip-hop, acid jazz and reggae releases. Take a look at the secondhand records as well – you may come across some Old School rap recordings at very interesting prices.

Vinylmania

**60 Carmine Street
(at Bedford St., B3)
☎ 924 72 23
Subway West 4th St.
Open Mon.-Sat. 11am-9pm,
Sun. 11am-7pm.**

As its name suggests, Vinylmania specialises in LPs, hip-hop, rap and jazz. Don't forget to pick up

some flyers to find out what's on in the way of concerts and events. And if you want to add to your CD collection, you can have a good rummage through the shelves located at the back of the shop.

Dance Tracks

**91 E 3rd Street
(at 1st Ave., B3)
☎ 260 87 29
Subway 2nd Ave.
Open Mon.-Thu. noon-9pm,
Fri. noon-10pm,
Sat. noon-8pm,
Sun. noon-7pm.**

Dance Tracks is a must. Listening points are available for you to try out the latest house, garage and other dance releases from Europe – and imported records are sold at cost price.

WORLD MUSIC, REGGAE AND ALTERNATIVE

J&R Music World

**23 Park Row (near
Beeckman St.)
☎ 238 90 00
Subway City Hall
or Chambers St.
Open Mon.-Sat. 9am-7pm
(Thu. to 7.30pm),
Sun. 10.30am-6.30pm.**

You won't be able to just pop briefly into this store – it's much too tempting. Although the atmosphere is not as cosy and intimate as in the smaller shops, the staff are very knowledgeable

and helpful and the prices often unbeatable (around $2-4 cheaper than elsewhere for new CDs). J&R is divided into two stores – one specialising in reggae and world music and the other selling all other genres (on two floors).

Generation Records

**210 Thompson Street
(between Bleecker
and 3rd St., B3)
☎ 254 11 00
Subway West 4th St.
Open Mon.-Thu. 11am-
10pm, Fri.-Sat. 11-1am,
Sun. noon-10pm.**

All kinds of alternative rock music on CD ($11-13) or vinyl, with excellent selections in the hardcore department, and the best (almost impossible to find elsewhere) imported records in all Greenwich Village.

SECONDHAND SHOPS AND MARKETS

New York is surely the best place to find secondhand clothes, which may have come straight from a couturier wardrobe or the attic of someone's grandmother. Retro accessories and secondhand dresses have become key essentials to mix with more up-to-date outfits.
For clothes-mad rummagers, it's a chance to track down rare items at reasonable prices. Get hunting!

SECONDHAND STORES

Alice Underground

**481 Broadway
(at Broome St., B3)
☎ 431 90 67
Subway Canal St.
Open every day
11am-7.30pm.**

A great selection of secondhand 1940s and 1950s clothes in good condition. The clothes are well organised and easy to find. and there are a few bins at the back of the shop for those who feel like a bit of a rummage. Bags, shoes and hats, and leather, suede and synthetic jackets – there's something here to suit all tastes, from glamorous to wild and whacky.

Harriet Love

**126 Prince Street
(between Wooster and Greene St., B3)
☎ 966 22 80
Subway Spring St.
Open every day 11am-7pm.**

Harriet Love will take you on a splendid nostalgic journey – it's one of the best shops for haute couture clothes of the 1930s and 1940s. The evening dresses are enchanting and in excellent condition, and all the retro jewellery is displayed with matching bags and more recent secondhand clothes.

Antique Boutique

**712-14 Broadway
(at Washington Place, B3)
☎ 460 88 30
Subway Astor Place
or 8th St.
Open every day
11am-9pm.**

This is one of the biggest secondhand clothes shops in the city, and is highly regarded by eccentric New Yorkers. It's divided into two stores, one for men and one for women, and you can find more or less anything here, from shoes and hats to jewellery and underwear. The styles are very original but the prices are a little high (around $40 on average).

Cheap Jack's

**841 Broadway (between
13th and 14th St., B3)
☎ 777 95 64 or 995 04 03
Subway 14th St.-Union
Square
Open Mon.-Sat. 11am-8pm
Sun. noon-7pm.**

This secondhand clothes shop has an outstanding stock of clothes from the 1930s and 1940s right up to the present day, with the 1970s look a speciality. There are rare items that will have fans of the 'Peace and Love' generation sighing with pleasure, including a fantastic collection of leather and denim bomber jackets, fur coats and bell-bottomed trousers as worn by the stars of

The Avengers.
There's just one hitch – the prices are a little on the steep side, but if you take the time to ferret about, you'll find a few reduced items for around $30.

What Comes Around Goes Around

**351 West Broadway
(at Broome St., B3)
☎ 343 93 03
Subway Spring St.
Open Mon.-Sat. 11am-8pm,
Sun. noon-7pm.**

One of the best places to buy good-quality secondhand clothes of every style from the 1880s to the 1970s, including a vast choice of accessories (jewellery, handbags, etc.) and the largest collection of vintage denim in the United States. You could well find the kitsch evening dress of your dreams here.

Screaming Mimis

**382 Lafayette
Street (B3)
☎ 677 64 64
Subway Astor
Place.
Open Mon.-Sat.
noon-8pm, Sun.
1-7pm.**

If you're looking for good quality, stylish clothes from the 1950s, 1960s and 1970s, this is the place to come. There's a huge choice of almost new shoes at excellent prices (around $20).

Young designers display their jewellery collections here, some of them kitsch and some rather unusual, together with new clothes with a retro feel. There's also a small section with some interesting beauty products.

SURPLUS AND THRIFT STORES

INA

**101 Thompson Street
(at Prince St., B3)
☎ 334 90 48
Subway Spring St.
Open every day noon-7pm.**

At INA, where the motto is 'recycling good fashion', you'll find lots of designer clothes owned by hard-up models sold to make ends meet. There's a good selection of evening dresses by well-known designers, all in excellent condition, from as little as $100, and an impressive range of shoes (with a tendency towards larger sizes). All the top designers are represented and you can also find coordinating accessories to complete your outfit at the back of the shop. At 262 Mott Street there's a branch which specialises in men's clothing only (☎ 334 22 10).

ARMY SURPLUS

ABC Army & Navy Store

2050 Lexington Avenue (at 124th St., B1)
☎ 722 22 85
Subway 125th St.
Open Mon.-Sat. 9am-6.30pm, Sun. 11am-5pm.

The ABC Army & Navy Store is ideal if you're looking for traditional army uniforms (fatigues, heavy woollen jumpers, hats and peaked caps), navy uniforms (long-sleeved striped T-shirts, etc.) or the camouflage gear that never seems to go out of fashion. These clothes are designed to keep out the bitter cold so this is the perfect place to come in the depths of winter.

Church Street Surplus

327 Church Street (B4)
☎ 226 52 80
Subway Canal St.
Open Mon.-Sat. 10.30am-6pm.

When you're on your way to the Canal Street markets, take a turn around Church Street Surplus and you may well come across a few treasures hidden away amongst the parkas, navy pullovers, and army and navy pants and jackets. Tucked away to one side is a small secondhand department selling mainly gorgeous and very wearable 1940s to 1960s dresses (around $20).

FLEA MARKETS

The Annex Antiques Fair & Flea Market

6th Avenue (from 24th to 27th St., B3)
Subway 23rd St.
Open Sat.-Sun. sunrise to sunset, all year round.
Entry charge $1.

This flea market has been very fashionable for some time now, for the simple reason that you can find just about everything here – 600 dealers selling clothes, jewellery, furniture, and sometimes marvellous collector's items. As if that weren't enough, there's even more to tempt you just a few steps away at 'The Garage' covered market

ENCORE

1132 Madison Avenue (B1)
☎ 879 28 50
Subway 86th St.
Open Mon., Wed., Fri.
10.30am-6.30pm,
Thu. 10.30am-7.30pm,
Sat. 10.30am-6pm, Sun.
noon-6pm.

People first started talking about Encore twenty years ago when the rumour went around that Jacqueline Kennedy Onassis was selling her wardrobe here. You can find clothes at incredible prices, such as Yves St Laurent dresses for $90 and Chanel suits for around $600. There's also a department entirely devoted to shoes, bags and other haute couture fashion accessories.

(112 W 25th Street, open every weekend 7am-5pm). Watch out for the prices, though, you'll be dealing with collectors.

Flea Market Columbus Avenue

Columbus Avenue (between 76th and 77th St., A1)
☎ 877 73 71
Subway 79th St.
Open Sun. 10am-6pm.
Entry free.

Don't miss this huge East Side indoor/outdoor market, also known as 'Greenflea', which is held on Sundays and always attracts vast crowds. All kinds of things are on sale here and there's even a section (Green market) selling fresh and organic produce. The open market is the most interesting. The air is filled with exotic smells, from Mexico, Bali or elsewhere, and many backpackers come here to sell craft items they've brought back from their travels.

Thrift & New Shoppe

602 9th Avenue (at 43rd St., A2)
☎ 265 30 87
Subway 42nd St.
Open Mon., Wed.-Sat.
8.30am-7pm, Sun.
noon-7pm.

It's difficult to see how so many things can fit into such a small shop. The bric-a-brac from the 1930s to the 1970s, some beautiful, some kitsch, includes vases, water jugs, pictures, globes and a multitude of china and porcelain. The owner is very friendly, too.

Nightlife Practicalities

A long with San Francisco, New York is the American city with the most hectic nightlife. Don't be disconcerted by the appearance of some of the people you come across in the course of the evening – you are in the city where anything goes and where free spirits of fashion roam. Don't be put off by the somewhat dilapidated and uninviting appearance of some of the bars and clubs – there'll be plenty of surprises in store inside.

WHERE TO GO FOR NEW YORK NIGHTLIFE

If you want to take in a Broadway show or a stage play during your stay, head for Times Square (42nd Street and Broadway). To dance the night away, take a trip to East Village. The four dance floors of Webster Hall (11th Street,

Headlines, Deadlines, Bylines

New York Times

The New York Times Morgue, 1896–1996

see p. 120) are a clubbers paradise. Greenwich Village is the mecca for jazz, with the two most famous clubs in New York – the Village Vanguard and Blue Note (see p. 122), where the genre never seems to go out of style. Finally, in SoHo, you have the choice between SOB's (see p. 123), which showcases music from all round the world, or one of the numerous late bars.

FINDING OUT WHAT'S ON DURING YOUR STAY

To find out what shows are playing during your stay in New York, check out www.broadway.com or www.offbroadwayonline.com. There are also several other websites with current listings, such as www.nyc.com and www.newyork.citysearch.com. You can also consult a number of publications, such

---

BUYING TICKETS

You can, of course, buy tickets at the theatre, though box offices often display sold out signs months in advance. If seats are still available, you can pay for them by cash, traveller's cheques or credit card. However, one of the best ways of buying tickets is to book by phone from home using a credit card, from an agency such as Telecharge (☎ 239 62 00), TicketMaster (☎ 307 41 00, www.ticketmaster.com) or TKTS (☎ 221 00 13). You'll be given all the relevant information and will be able to book the seats instantly. The tickets will then be sent to you direct. Don't forget, you'll be charged a booking fee of approximately $6 per ticket. For show information, try NYC/On Stage (☎ 768 18 18).

as the *New York Times* (which has a very interesting Sunday supplement), the *New York Press*, the *Village Voice,* which is indispensable for the most avant-garde events, and *Time Out Magazine*. The Civic Center of New York publishes a complete list of forthcoming events several months in advance and is an invaluable source of information. Finally, check out the flyers you can pick up in every music store and trendy shop as they sometimes give a reduction on the price of admission to evening events.

FINDING YOUR WAY

Next to each address in the Shopping and Nightlife and Tours sections we have given its location on the map of New York on pages 78-79.

REDUCED-PRICE SHOWS

Reduced-price tickets for shows (25 to 50% reduction) are available on the same day from the ticket offices of **TKTS** (Broadway and 47th St., ☎ 221 00 13), but the choice is limited, credit cards aren't accepted and the queues are quite long. Make sure you arrive at least an hour before opening time to be certain of getting seats (open every day 3pm-8pm). **TicketMaster** also sells reduced-price tickets. Valid the same day, they're on sale in the kiosk located inside Bloomingdale's department store.

For concerts, dance and theatre, **Music & Dance Booth** (42nd St. and 6th Ave.) offers half-price tickets valid for the same evening.

However, they don't accept credit cards.

Lastly, *Twofers* (two tickets for the price of one) and cut-price vouchers are available for a wide choice of theatre seats from **NYC's Official Visitor Information Center**, (☎ 484 12 22, www.nycvisit.com).

LOW-BUDGET EVENINGS

Many concerts, dance performances and other events are free. These take place in parks and gardens (in Central Park in the summer) or in churches. A list of forthcoming events can be found in the *New York Times, Village Voice* or *Time Out*. This is also true of many operas (those at the Metropolitan Opera House are definitely well recommended, ☎ 362 60 00, www.metopera.com). There are free jazz concerts every Sunday afternoon at St Peter's church (Lexington Ave. and 54th St., ☎ 935 22 00).

SAFETY

New York has become considerably safer of late and the 'Big Apple' is now far less dangerous than some of the other big American cities, such as Washington, Detroit and Los Angeles. As anywhere, you simply need to use your

common sense. Don't tempt fate, don't leave your valuables or passport on show, don't walk around with all your money on you and try to act naturally and seem sure of yourself. If you mean to go out late, always take a taxi rather than the subway.

ALCOHOL AND TOBACCO

You must be over 21 to drink alcohol and be admitted to certain clubs in New York. Many bars will ask you to provide photo ID in order to check your age, so don't forget to keep yours on you.

As of July 2003 cigarette smoking is strictly forbidden in bars, restaurants and public buildings, including cinemas, theatres and concert halls, and as soon as you cross the threshold you're obliged to put them out.

ALTERNATIVE WAYS OF SEEING NEW YORK

Guided tours

Harlem Spirituals

690 8th Avenue (between
43th and 44th St., A2)
☎ 391 09 00
www.harlemspirituals.com
Subway 42nd St.-Port Auth.
Tickets $39-75

These tours are an ideal way to discover Harlem. Great any day of the week, they are fantastic on Sundays, when you can eat brunch to the sound of a gospel choir. Booking is essential. They also offer evening 'jazz' tours.

Gray Line

Port Authority Bus Terminal
8th Avenue (at 42nd St., A2)
☎ 1 800 669 00 51
www.graylinenewyork.com

Subway 42nd St.-Port
Authority
Daily 7.45am-8pm.
Tickets $25-$69.

One of the largest tour companies in New York, offering over twenty guided tours with English-speaking guides. If you have the time, there's a 9-hour grand tour, including lunch.

Hassidic Walking Tours

Meeting point:
305 Kingston Ave., Brooklyn
(between Eastern Parkway
and Union Ave., off map)
☎ 1 800 838 86 87 or
☎ (718) 953 52 44
www.jewishtours.com
Subway Kingston Ave.
Sun.-Thu. 10am-10.30pm.
Tickets $36 (children $18).

There's always been a large Hassidic community in New York and you can discover all about their life and customs on this fascinating 3-hour tour, which includes a visit to a synagogue and lunch in a kosher deli. Booking essential.

New York Apple Tours

Empire State Building
350 5th Avenue
(at 34th St., B2)
☎ 1 800 876 98 68
Subway 34th St.
Daily 9am-5pm.
Tickets $25-81.

Double-decker buses leave regularly (every hour or half-hour) and the tour lasts around two hours. For a really good view, sit on the top deck.

A bird's eye view of New York

Liberty Helicopter Tours

VIP Heliport, West Side
Highway (at W 30th St., A2)
☎ 967 45 50 or
☎ 465 89 05
(recorded information)
Subway 34th St.-Penn Stn.
daily 9am-9pm.
Tickets $56-162.

If you want to avoid the crowds and the heavy traffic, Liberty is reputed to be the best company for seeing the city from the air. There's a choice of itineraries, all of which include a flight over Ellis Island, the Statue of Liberty and Downtown.

Boat trips

The Petrel

Battery Park (A4)
☎ 1 877 693 61 31 (info line)
Subway Cortlandt St.
Sailing tours May-Oct.

This magnificent sailing ship has several embarkations a day from its berth next to the Staten Island Ferry. Booking essential.

Circle Line

Pier 83, W 42nd Street
(at 12th Ave., A2)
☎ 563 32 00
www.circleline.com
Subway 42nd St.-Port Auth.
Departures every 45 mins
(3 hour tour), 10am-4pm.
Tickets $25 (adults),
$12 (children under 12).

From April to November, Circle Line offers $1^1/_2$- or 3-hour boat trips along Manhattan Island. From June to August, there's a two-hour night trip to see the port lit up. If you're not afraid of getting wet, try *The Beast* (April-Sept., ☎ 630 88 88), and travel at high speed for 30 minutes.

Bateaux New York

Suite 200A,
Chelsea Piers, Pier 62 (A3)
☎ 352 13 66
www.bateauxnewyork.com
Subway 23rd St.
Daily noon-2pm, 7-10pm
Tickets $45 and $120.

Bateaux New York specialises in lunch and dinner cruises. After your meal, the boat becomes a dance floor. It's a magical way to travel. The curved glass walls and ceiling allow you to watch the skyline and the stars.

Staten Island Ferry

Battery Park (A4)
☎ 718 815 (BOAT)
Subway Cortlandt St.
Daily, 24 hours a day.

These ferries take suburban dwellers across the Bay of New York to Staten Island leaving every half hour. It's easily the cheapest and most popular boat trip – the crossing is free! At that sort of price, why wouldn't you take advantage of it?

New York in 25 minutes!

New York Skyride

Empire State Building,
2nd floor, 350 5th Ave.
(at 34th St., B2)
☎ 279 97 77
www.skyride.com
Subway 34th St.
Open every day 10am-10pm.
Tickets $15.50 (adults),
$12.50 (children).

This 25-minute 3D film show takes you into every corner of the Big Apple without leaving your seat. If you haven't a minute to call your own on a short trip to New York, this is a great way to see the city in record time!

Bicycle tours

Central Park Bicycle Tours

Meeting point:
2 Columbus Circle (between 59th St. and Broadway, A2)
☎ 541 87 59
www.centralparkbiketour.com
Subway 59th St.-Columbus Circle
Daily Apr.-Dec. 10am, 1pm and 4pm, Jan.-March by appt.
Tickets $20-30.

This leisurely 2-hour tour of Central Park is a great way to discover this famous area and to experience the countryside in the heart of the city.

Statue of Liberty & Ellis Island Ferry
CIRCLE LINE

LATE NIGHT BARS

There are many late night bars and clubs in New York – after all this is the 'city that never sleeps'. People tend to eat early and go out for a drink or to listen to some music later.

West Village

Art Bar

52 8th Avenue (A3)
☎ 727 02 44
Subway 14th St.
Open every day 4pm-4am.

Having made your way through the first room, with its amazing mural of *The Last Supper*, with Jim Morrison as Christ, and Madonna, Andy Warhol and Marilyn Monroe as apostles, you'll come to a cosy room lit by candles, with deep armchairs, drapes and potted palms. You can relax, kick off your shoes and have a meal. Prices are cheap, with a wide variety of dishes and drinks on offer.

Bar d'O

29 Bedford Street (A3)
☎ 627 15 80
Subway Christopher St.
Open every day 7pm-3am.

This bar has a reputation for its talented drag queens and their inimitable renderings of classic American songs. Warm and comfortable, it's an interesting place that's well worth a detour.

Greenwich Village

Zinc Bar

**90 W Houston Street
(at La Guardia Place, A3)**
☎ 477 83 37
www.zincbar.com
Subway Houston St.
**Open daily 6pm-3.30am
(to 4am at the weekend).**

Head down the steep stairs and through the velvet curtains into this long bar, divided into two rooms – the one at the back is particularly atmospheric with

its Mediterranean-style interior. There's live music every evening from 10.30pm – a mix of jazz, Brazilian, Cuban and African sounds – and poetry readings at 6.30pm on Sunday.

Merc Bar

151 Mercer Street (between Prince and Houston, B3)
☎ 966 27 27
Subway Prince St.
**Open Mon.-Tue. 5pm-2am,
Wed.-Thu 5pm-3am, Fri.-Sat.
5pm-4am, Sun. 6pm-2am.**

A mountain chalet decor greets Merc Bar's eclectic clientele, who range from Wall Street yuppies to East Village artists. The music is excellent and not too loud, so you can enjoy a very pleasant and comfortable evening here.

Pravda

281 Lafayette Street (near Houston St., B3)
☎ 334 50 15
**Subway Broadway-Lafayette
Open Mon.-Thu. 5pm-
3am, Fri.-Sat. 5pm-4am,
Sun. 5pm-1am.**

A large, trendy bar-restaurant, decorated to look like a secret KGB rendezvous. Signs in Cyrillic characters accentuate the Russian decor and over 70 different brands of vodka are on sale, with almost as many martinis. The young clientele also comes to sample salmon, blinis and caviar.

East Village, Astor Place

Beauty Bar

231 E 14th Street (B3)
☎ 539 13 89
**Subway 3rd Ave.
Open Mon.-Fri. 5pm-4am,
Sat.-Sun. 7pm-4am.**

A former beauty salon, as you can tell from the sign outside, this bar has a decor dating back about thirty years. Here you can sip a delicious cocktail sitting

under an enormous hairdryer while listening to old pop songs. Definitely the place to let your hair down.

Fez

**Under Time Café
380 Lafayette Street,
(at Great Jones St., B3)
☎ 533 26 80
www.feznyc.com
Subway Broadway-Lafayette
Open Sun.-Thu. 6pm-2am,
Fri.-Sat. 6pm-4am.**

The Fez is a Moroccan bar with a young clientele and a beatnik air, a sharp contrast with the chromium-plated Time Café above. You can sink into deep sofas or stretch out on huge pouffes arranged around the heavy wooden tables with metal tops. The music is a mix of dance, funk and 80s hits and there's

always a great atmosphere. There are also live poetry readings and the occasional jazz concert. Great cocktails.

Barmacy

**538 E 14th Street
(between Avenues A and B)
☎ 228 22 40
Subway 1st Ave.
Open Mon.-Fri. 5.30pm-4am,
Sat.-Sun. 7.30pm-4am.**

The barmaids wear nurses' uniforms, and the cocktails are 'New-York strong' (just what the doctor ordered), dressed up as medicine with names such as 'Pepto Bismal'. There's a great atmosphere in this former pharmacy with a spacious room out back. The DJ plays rock music.

Lower East Side

Max Fish

**178 Ludlow Street (between Houston and Stanton St., B3)
☎ 529 39 59
Subway Second Ave.
Open every day 5.30pm-4am.**

Eccentric or insomniac artists, writers and musicians congregate at Max Fish, a trendy bar with one of the best CD jukeboxes

in the city. You may even come across a few celebrities (Johnny Depp is occasionally seen), who come here to enjoy the beer ($2.50 per pint).

Lansky Lounge

**104 Norfolk Street
(between Delancey and
Rivington St., B3)
☎ 677 94 89
Subway Delancey St.
Open Sun.-Thu. 6pm-2am,
Fri.-Sat. 6pm-4am.**

This bar was a speakeasy during the Prohibition and is named after Meyer Lansky, a Jewish gangster who lived in the neighbourhood – hence the 1940s decor. From 10pm a DJ does his stuff, with really good soul music evenings held on the first Thursday of the month.

NIGHTCLUBS

Always on the lookout for something new, New York offers plenty of choice for sensation-hungry clubbers seeking new experiences. Some clubs have become institutions, while others flourish and vanish in a matter of months. For the latest information, consult the *Village Voice* or *Time Out*.

Tunnel

**220 12th Avenue
(at 27th St., A3)
☎ 695 46 82
Subway 14th St.-8th Ave.
Open Fri. 10pm-noon, Sat.
11pm-noon , Sun. 10pm-4am
Entry charge $20.**

A huge club with an impressive decor. Unisex toilets (restrooms) with a bar and seating, a café, a 'cosmic cave' decorated by American artist Kenny Scharf (fake fur from floor to ceiling, lava-lamps and Internet terminals), as well as 7 rooms with 5 DJs playing a variety of music. There's always something interesting going on here.

Sound Lab

The experimental shows organised by Sound Lab are an absolute must. These visual and sound performances presented by the best DJs on the world music scene are always impressive and are among the most popular events taking place here. For information about these itinerant evenings, call the information line advertised on flyers available in all the trendy shops in the city.

The Cooler

416 W 14th Street (between 9th and 10th Ave., A3)
☎ 229 07 85
Subway 14th St. or 8th Ave.
Open every day 9.30pm-4am.
Entry charge $8-15.

In addition to concerts, the Cooler offers excellent jungle

and techno evenings. Try the special nights on Tuesdays (10pm-4am), organised by the brilliant Liquid Sky Production – an explosion in sound and light of trance, techno and jungle.

The Roxy

515 W 18th Street (between 10th and 11th Ave., A3)
☎ 645 51 56
www.roxynyc.com
Subway 8th Ave. and 14th St.
Open every day 8pm-2am (Wed. reserved for rollerskaters/rollerbladers).
Entry charge $10-$15.

One of the most fashionable places in the city. A wild, extravagant crowd of transvestites, drag queens and ravers get together on the dance floor, which shakes to the beat of house and techno, as well as favourite tunes from the 1960s, 1970s and 1980s. The decor is decadent, with velvet draperies and neo-Classical statues. Wednesday nights there's a roller disco, while Friday night is party night and Saturday sees one of the best gay nights in town. They also host one-off events and concerts.

Webster Hall

125 E 11th Street (between 3rd and 4th Ave., B3)
☎ 353 16 00
Subway 14th St.-Union Sq.
Open Thu.-Sat. 11pm-4am.
Entry charge $30.

The archetypal themed disco, with four enormous dance floors and a different style of music on each one. From pounding techno and acid jazz to rock and reggae, there's something to suit every taste, as well as a stage for Thursday concerts. There's even a wig shop in the basement, in case you feel the need to do your clubbing incognito!

Nell's

246 W 14th Street (between 7th and 8th Ave., A3)
☎ 675 15 67
Subway 14th St.
Open every day 10pm-4am except Mon. (6pm-midnight).
Entry charge $10-15.

The two floors of Nell's are a magnet for New York clubbers thirsty for funk, soul, rap, etc. The programmes change every night and guarantee Nell's a regular and very varied clientele. The basement is taken over by hip-hop or R&B fans and the atmosphere is infectious. Higher up, the Victorian-style sitting-room, complete with sofas and ornate woodwork allows you to listen to jazz numbers in an altogether calmer atmosphere, as well as enjoy a late supper.

Vinyl

**6 Hubert Street
(between Hudson and
Greenwich St., A4)
☎ 343 13 79
Subway Canal St. or
Franklin St.
Open Fri.-Sat. from
midnight, Sun. 3-11pm.**

One of the best venues to hear the latest sounds. The Body & Soul tea party on Sunday afternoon is a New York must, when resident DJs spin cutting-edge and classic house with frequent appearances by guest vocalists. A vast space with a diverse crowd.

Organic Grooves

**For information and
location ☎ 439 11 47.**

For the past 7 years the Organic Grooves Collective has held Friday night parties all over New York City. Created by a collective of DJs and musicians, the music blends live instrumentation with original tracks, and mixes tribal drum beats with contemporary sampling techniques and electronics to create a unique, pretty off beat sound.

Sound Factory

**618 W 46th Street (between
11th and 12th Ave., A2)
☎ 643 07 28
Subway 50th St.**

The legendary Sound Factory reopened its doors in 1997 and although DJ Junior Vasquez no longer does his stuff in the evenings, it's still a very popular spot. It has everything you might

expect from a club; a huge disco ball, several floors of good music and an interesting decor. The Friday night party is the most popular event. Those who survive until breakfast time are served coffee, cookies and fruit. The proposed fourth floor may even end up with a hot tub.

CONCERTS

Every evening, dozens of concerts take place in New York, covering a wide variety of music genres such as classical, jazz, techno and rock. You'll be spoilt for choice. To find out what's playing at the various concert halls, consult the *Village Voice* or *Time Out*.

Pop and rock

CBGB

**315 Bowery
(at Bleecker St., B3)
☎ 982 40 52
www.cbgb.com**

**Subway Bleecker St.
and Broadway-Lafayette
Open Mon.-Fri. 7.30pm-4am,
Sat. and Sun. 8.30pm-4am.
Entry charge $5-10.**

Over the past thirty years, CBGB has become the home of American punk. It stages performances by some excellent groups (new wave, hard rock, etc.), and you won't be disappointed – the shows are always first-rate. If you really don't like the music, you can always take a look at the gallery in the annexe. The first band comes on around 7pm.

Wetlands

**161 Hudson Street
(at Hubert St., A4)
☎ 386 36 00
Subway Franklin St.
or Canal St.
Opening times and entry
charge are variable.**

Neo-hippy to the last, this club will take you back to your school-days, or those of your parents. An old VW bus takes pride of place next to the dance floor, full of brochures about the latest waste recycling programme or next meeting of Greenpeace. Put on some loose clothes and commune with the youth of New York to music by bands such as Phish.

Jazz

Village Vanguard

178 7th Avenue South
(at Perry St., A3)
☎ 255 40 37
Subway 14th St.
Open Mon.-Wed. 8.30pm-
2am, Thu., Sun. 8.30pm-1am,
Fri.-Sat. 8.30pm-2.30am.
Entry charge $25-30

The Village Vanguard hasn't
changed in thirty years. All the
most famous jazz musicians,
such as Pharaoh Sanders, John
Coltrane and Miles Davis, have
performed here. These stars
have left their mark, which is
why the club has become a
New York institution. Monday
nights are reserved for the
Vanguard jazz band.

Iridium Jazz Club

1650 Broadway
(at 51st St., A2)
☎ 582 21 21
www.iridiumjazzclub.com
Subway 50th St.
Open Fri.-Sat. 7pm-2am,
Sun.-Thu. 5pm-midnight.
Entry charge $20-30.

Iridium has moved from the
Lincoln Center to a new location
in this historic jazz neighbourhood. It now boasts an
excellent sound system, a
programme of some of the
hottest acts (a mix of the famous
and not yet so famous), a

BLUE NOTE

131 W 3rd Street
(between 6th Ave. and
McDougal St.)
☎ 475 85 92
www.bluenote.net/newyork
Subway W 4th St.
Open Sun.-Thu. 7pm-2am,
Fri., Sat. 7pm-4am.
Entry charges $10-65.

The Blue Note is one of the
best jazz clubs in New York.
It offers excellent programmes
with the biggest stars – Sarah
Vaughan and Ray Charles have
both performed here, and you
may even see one of them turn
up unexpectedly for the pleasure
of playing a few numbers. Jazz
Brunch is served on Sundays
(11.30am-4pm), with shows at
12.30 and 2.30pm. A smart club
and a little pricey.

selection of up-market dishes and an extensive wine list. Show times are 8pm and 10pm (with another at 11.30pm Fri. and Sat.). The popular Sunday Jazz Brunch Buffet takes place from 11.30am to 3pm ($16.95).

Latin American and world music

SOBs (Sounds of Brazil)
**204 Varick Street
(at Houston St., A3)
☎ 243 49 40
Subway Houston St.
Open Mon. 5pm-3am,
Tue.-Sat. 8pm-3am.
Entry charge $10-30.**

This club stages concerts of Latin American and African music, samba, soca and salsa, as well as reggae, bhangra and Haitian sounds. There are sometimes also live performances by funk and soul stars of the 1970s.

Classical music and opera

Carnegie Hall
**154 W 57th Street
(at 7th Ave., A2)
☎ 247 78 00
Subway 59th St.-
Columbus Circle
Open Mon.-Sat. 11am-6pm,
Sun. noon-6pm.
Tickets $20-90.**

Tchaikovsky directed the inaugural concert here in 1891. Despite a demolition order issued in 1960, the hall still stages a varied programme of concerts, with performances by stars from all over the world, from Liza Minelli to Neil Sedaka, as well as piano recitals, choral works, chamber music, symphony orchestras and jazz groups. A new auditorium is presently under construction and is due to open in 2003.

Metropolitan Opera House
**Lincoln Center
(between Columbus
and Amsterdam Ave.,
62nd-65th St., A1)
☎ 362 60 00
Subway 66th St.**

**Open Mon.-Sat. 10am-8pm,
Sun. noon-6pm.
Tickets $24-225.**

The Metropolitan Opera House, boasting tapestries by Marc Chagall, is a respected institution housing the biggest opera company in New York, the Metropolitan Opera Company. The tickets are very expensive (even though you don't always have a good view of the stage) and you have to buy them in advance. You could try your luck for a seat in the Family Circle on the day of the performance.

Amato Opera Company
**319 Bowery (at 2nd St., B3)
☎ 228 82 00
Subway 2nd Ave.
Tickets $20-30.**

If you haven't managed to see the Amato Opera Company performing free in the parks in August, buy your tickets now. This is where you'll discover the stars of tomorrow. Most of the former members of the chorus now sing with the Metropolitan or New York Opera. The fine repertoire includes Baroque, Romantic and Classical works, from Mozart to Verdi (between Sept. and June).

DANCE

There are two main dance seasons – from September to February and March to June. Dance thrives in New York, from the big classical companies of the Lincoln Center to the small experimental groups.

Merce Cunningham Dance Company

11th floor, 55 Bethune Street (between Washington and West St., A3)
☎ 255 82 40
Subway 14th St.
Tickets $10-30.

Be prepared for a longish walk as the Merce Cunningham Studio is in Greenwich Village. However, it's always well worth the effort, as the 'master's' dance studio regularly stages performances by the company, as well as works by gifted young choreographers. There's a 'no shoes'

policy in the upstairs room. For more information, call the Foundation on ☎ 255 82 40.

Joyce Theater

175 8th Avenue
(at 19th St., A3)
☎ 242 08 00
Subway 18th St. or 23rd St.
Tickets $20-40.

The 472-seat Joyce Theatre has been transformed into a pleasant, intimate setting for performances by small New York companies of recognised talent. Eliot Feld began his career here in a piece by Balanchine and his present company, Feld Ballet, is based at the theatre. Meredith Monk and the Erick Hawkins

Dance Company have also performed here. The Joyce Theater's summer programme is always interesting and full of up-and-coming talent.

Dance Theater Workshop

Bessie Schönberg Theater
219 W 19th Street (between 7th and 8th St., A3)
☎ 924 00 77
Subway 18th St. and 23rd St.

You won't find any point shoes and tutus here. The Dance Theater Workshop has moved into the field of experimental dance and the group tirelessly searches for new ways of using space. The theatre is one of the best organised places for this type of performance, and provides a wealth of opportunities. In 2001 the theatre underwent a massive rebuilding project which doubled the existing space.

This theatre, with its revolving stage, was built in 1907 by actor, director and theatrical designer David Belasco. Its decorative interior includes Tiffany glass.

Eugene O'Neill Theater

230 W 49th Street (between Broadway and 8th Ave., A2)
☎ 239 62 00 (agency)
Subway 50th St.

It was here that Arthur Miller's *All My Sons* was performed for the first time. Nowadays, plays alternate with musicals.

Virginia Theater

245 W 52nd Street (between Broadway and 8th Ave., A2)
☎ 239 62 00 (agency)
Subway 50th St.

In 1923 Shaw's *Caesar and Cleopatra* was first performed here. Charming and elegant.

City Center Theater

131 W 55th Street (between 6th and 7th Ave., A2)
☎ 247 04 30
Subway 7th Ave.
tickets $25-75.

Before the Lincoln Center changed the cultural geography of New York, the City Center Theater was home to the New York City Ballet and American Ballet Theater. The theatre has retained its charm and stages excellent performances by such companies as those of Merce Cunningham, Martha Graham and Alvin Alley.

THEATRE AND VARIETY

The energy generated in New York filters through to its theatre productions, which fall into three main categories: 'Broadway' – all the big crowd-pulling shows, 'Off Broadway' – smaller theatres staging anything from comedies to one-man shows, and 'Off-Off Broadway', which is experimental theatre and the work of young,

avant-garde companies. Many of these groups aren't on the phone. For information, call Telecharge (☎ 239 62 00), or consult *Time Out* or the *New York Times*.

Broadway

Belasco Theater

111 W 44th Street (between Broadway and 8th Ave., A2)
Subway 42nd St. and Times Square.

Off Broadway

The Public Theater

425 Lafayette Street (between Astor Place and E 4th St., B3)
☎ 260 24 00
Subway Astor Place and 8th St.

This theatre complex housing six different companies stages productions by new American authors and actors. *A Chorus Line* and *Hair* were first created here before being taken onto Broadway.

Index

This guide was written by **Anne-Catherine Sore** with **Thierry Chauvaud** and **Hélène Firquet**.
New edition revised by **Sandrine Rabardeau** with assistance from **Caroline Boissy**, **Jean-Pierre Marenghi** and **Magali Vidal**.
Design: **Chrystel Arnould**. Cartography: **Cyrille Suss**.
UK edition translated and edited by **Margaret Rocques**.
Additional research and assistance: **Jenny Piening**, **Ryan Tozzi**, **Jane Moseley** and **Christine Bell**.

We have done our best to ensure the accuracy of the information contained in this guide. However, addresses, phone numbers, opening times etc. inevitably do change from time to time, so if you find a discrepancy please do let us know. You can contact us at: HachetteTravel@philips-maps.co.uk or write to us at the address below.

Hachette Travel Guides provide independent advice. The authors and compilers do not accept any remuneration for the inclusion of any addresses in these guides.

Please note that we cannot accept any responsibility for any loss, injury or inconvenience sustained by anyone as a result of any information or advice contained in this guide.

Photo acknowledgements

Inside pages: **Bernard Grilly**: pp. 11 (t.l., c.r.), 12 (c.r.), 13 (b.l.), 14 (c.l.), 15 (t.l.), 16 (b.l.), 17, 19 (t.l.), 20 (t.), 21 (t.l., t.r., b.r.), 22 (t., c.l., b.), 23 (c.c.), 24 (c.r.), 25 (t.r., t.c., b.r.), 26 (c.l.), 27 (b.l., b.r.), 29 (c.l.), 35 (b.r.), 39 (t.l.), 41 (t.l.), 42 (b.l.), 50 (b.r.), 56 (c.l.), 60 (c.r.), 61 (t.r., c.l.), 62 (c.r.), 63 (t.r., c.l.), 70 (b.l.), 74 (t.r.), 75 (t.c.), 82 (c.l., c.r.), 85 (t.l.), 89 (b.l.), 91 (c.r.), 95 (c.l.), 97 (t.r.), 101 (c.r.), 104 (b.r.), 105 (t.r., b.l.), 106 (c.r.), 108 (b.r.), 110 (c.r.), 112, 120 (c.r.). **Heidrun Holzfeind**: pp. 14 (c.c.), 18 (c.l., c.r., b.l.), 20 (c.r., b.l.), 21 (c.c.), 23 (b.l.), 26 (t., b.), 27 (t.l., c.c.), 40, 47 (t.l.), 48 (b.l.), 57 (b.c.), 75 (b.r.), 76 (t.r.), 80 (c.l.), 81 (c.l.), 87 (c.r.), 88 (c.l.), 90 (b.l.), 95 (b.r.), 98 (t.), 99 (b.l.), 103 (c.l., b.c.), 106 (t., b.l.), 107 (c.l.), 108 (c.c., b.l.), 109 (t.r.), 116, 119, 121 (c.r.). **Laurent Parrault**: pp. 2, 3, 10 (c.l., b.l.), 11 (b.r.), 12 (t.r.), 13 (c.c.), 18 (t.r.), 19 (t.r., b.c.), 22 (c.c.), 23 (t.r.), 25 (c.l., c.c.), 28, 29 (c.r., b.), 34, 35 (t.l., c.c., b.l.), 36, 37 (c.l., c.r.), 38 (b.l.), 39 (c.l., b.r.), 41 (c.r., b.c., b.r.), 42 (b.r.), 43 (t.c., c.l.), 44 (c.r.), 45 (t.r., b.r.), 46 (c.r.), 47 (c.c.), 48 (c.l.), 49, 51 (b.), 52, 53 (c.r.), 54, 57 (c.r.), 58, 59 (t.l., c.c., t.r.), 60 (b.l.), 61 (b.r.), 62 (c.l.), 63 (t.c., c.r., b.c.), 66 (b.l., b.r.), 67 (t.l., b.c.), 72 (c.l.), 73, 76 (c.c.), 77 (t.r., c.l.), 80 (t., b.c.), 81 (t.l., t.r., b.c.), 82 (t.), 83 (t.c., c.l., b.), 84 (t.r., b.), 85 (t.), 86, 87 (c.r.), 88 (t., c.c.), 89 (b.r.), 91 (t.l., b.l., b.r.), 92 (t., b.r.), 93, 94 (t., b.c.), 95 (b.l.), 96, 97 (t.c., c.c., b.r.), 99 (c.r.), 100, 101 (c.c., b.r.), 102 (t.l., t.r., c.c., b.r.), 103 (c.r.), 104 (t., c.c., c.l.), 105 (c.l.), 107 (b.r.), 108 (t.), 109 (c.l.), 110 (t.), 111 (t.r., c.r., b.), 114, 115, 120 (b.), 122 (b.), 123 (t.l., b.c.), 124 (t.r., t.l., c.c., b.l.), 125 (t.l., c.c., c.r., b.l., b.r.), 126, 127, 128, 129, 130 (t., c.r.), 131 (c.c., b.l.), 132, 133, 136, 137. **Éric Guillot**: pp. 56 (b.c.), 59 (b.r.), 65 (b.r.), 74 (c.c.), 77 (b.c.), 83 (c.c.), 84 (c.l., c.r.), 87 (c.c.). **Patrick Meagher**: pp. 12 (b.l., b.r.), 19 (c.r.), 24 (b.l.), 51 (c.c.), 61 (b.l.), 92 (c.c.), 107 (t.). **Christian Sarramon**: p. 65 (c.r.). **P.J. Vitakis**: pp. 70 (t.r.), 80 (c.r.), 94 (c.l.), 118. **Hémisphères**: **Laurent Borgey-Loyer**: pp. 15 (c.c.), 23 (b.r.), 24 (b.r.), 25 (b.l.), 43 (c.r.), 44 (b.l.), 47 (b.l.), 48 (b.r.), 53 (c.r.), 70 (c.r.), 71 (c.r.), 75 (c.l.), 90 (c.c.), 92 (b.r.), 102 (b.l.), 113, 120 (t.l.), 121 (t.l.), 122 (t.c., c.r.), 123 (c.r.). **Bertrand Gardel**: pp. 37 (t.l.), 50 (c.l.). **Laurent Giraudou**: pp. 10 (c.r.), 14 (t., b.), 16 (c.r.), 24 (t.), 39 (c.c.), 44 (c.l.), 46 (b.l.), 56 (c.r.). **J.P. Lescourret**: pp. 11 (c.l.), 13 (t.). **Bertrand Rieger**: pp. 64 (c.l., c.r.), 66 (c.l.), 67 (c.l., c.r.). **Ask Images**: **S. Attal**: p. 57 (t.l.). **Martha Cooper**: p. 64 (b.l.). **Degas**: p. 65 (t.r.). **S. Fautre**: p. 51 (c.r.). **Joe Viesti**: p. 37 (t.r.). **Photothèque Hachette**: pp. 10 (t.r.), 15 (b.r., *Portraits de M. Monroe* by A. Warhol, ADAGP, Paris, 1997), 16 (t.), 55 (b.r.), 130 (b.l.), 131 (t.). **Pop Shop, Alex Cao**: pp. 29 (t.r.), 53 (t.l.). **Rainbow Room Restaurant**: p. 38 (c.r.). **The Frick Collection, New York**: p. 134 (c.l., c.r.). **Richard di Liberto**: p. 43 (b.r.). **John Bigelow Taylor**: pp. 125 (b.c.), 134 (b.l., t.r.). **Museum of American Folk Art**: p. 45 (c.c., b.l.). **Village Chess Shop**: p. 47 (b.r.). **F.G.B**: p. 50 (b.l.). **Pop Shop, Tseng Kwong Chi, courtesy: estate of Keith Haring**: p. 53 (b.l.). **Jerry's**: p. 55 (c.). **Mercer Hotel**: p. 70 (t.l.). **Hôtel Franklin**: p. 72 (t.r.). **Hôtel Shoreham**: p. 72 (b.l.). **The Exclusive Oilily Store**: p. 89 (t.r.). **Museum of Modern Art**: pp. 95 (c.c.), 98 (b.), 99 (t.l.). **Jewish Museum's Cooper Shop**: p. 99 (b.c.). **Love Saves the Day**: p. 103 (t.r.). **Fez at Time Café**: p. 117 (t.r.). **American Museum of Natural History, D. Finnin**: p. 125 (t.r.). **Craig Chesek**: p. 135 (c.l.); **Scott Frances**: p. 135 (t.r.); **J. Beckett/D. Finnin**: p. 135 (b.c.); **J. Beckett**: p. 135 (b.r.).

Front cover: **Stéphane Frances, Hémisphères**: c.r.; **Jeff Hunter, Image Bank**: t.c. (figure); **Laurent Giraudou, Hémisphères**: t.r., b.l.; **Bernard Grilly**: c.l., b.r., t.r., b.l.; **S.r.P., A.l.E Fotostock**: c.r., (figure); **Claire Dubois, Stock Image**: b.c., (figure). *Back cover*: **Bernard Grilly**: b.l.; **Laurent Parrault**: c. (glasses); **Bertrand Gardel, Hémisphères**: t.r.; **Laurent Giraudaou, Hémisphères**: c.l.

Illustrations Pascal Garnier   **Cartography** © Hachette Tourisme

STAYING ON A LITTLE LONGER

If you're staying on and would like to try some new places, the following pages give you a wide choice of hotels, restaurants and bars, listed by district with addresses.

Although you can just turn up at some restaurants and have a meal (except in the most prestigious establishments), don't forget to book your hotel several days in advance (see page 68). Enjoy your stay!

(see page 68)

Please note that the prices given should serve as a guide only and are subject to change.

The hotels listed in the following pages are classified by district and, within each district, by price. The letter in brackets after each hotel name indicates the price range per night for a double room without breakfast, but please note these prices should serve as a guide only:

A – under $150
B – $150–$250
C – over $250

For more information, see pp. 68-69.

Around SoHo

Off SoHo Suites (A)
11 Rivington Street
(near the Bowery)
☎ 979 98 08
☎ 1 800 633 76 46
(in US only)
𝐅 979 98 01
www.offsoho.com
The rooms are large and inexpensive and are located in the East Village and the Lower East Side.

Holiday Inn Downtown (B)
138 Lafayette Street
(at Canal St.)
☎ 966 88 98
𝐅 966 39 33
www.holidayinn-nyc.com
Relatively large rooms and a young clientele in Chinatown, very close to SoHo.

Greenwich

Larchmont Hotel (A)
27 W 11th Street
(at 5th Ave.)
☎ 989 93 33
𝐅 989 94 96
www.larchmonthotel.com
A small, well-kept hotel with a safari-style decor. No private bathrooms.

Between 14th Street and 42nd Street

Carlton Arms (A)
160 E 25th Street
(at Lexington Ave.)
☎ 679 06 80
𝐅 684 83 37

Simple but low-priced hotel. Each room has a different themed decor and an original wall painting specially commissioned from an artist. A fun choice for bargain hunters.

Chelsea Inn (A)
46 W 17th Street
(at 6th Ave.)
☎ 645 89 89
𝐅 645 19 03
A 19th-century townhouse with a choice of suites or single rooms with private or shared bathrooms and kitchenettes.

Chelsea Pines Inn (A)
317 W 14th Street
(at 9th Ave.)
☎ 929 10 23
𝐅 620 56 46
23 comfortable rooms in a small hotel decorated with gay film posters.

Chelsea Savoy Hotel (A)
204 W 23rd Street
(at 8th Ave.)
☎ 929 93 53
𝐅 741 63 09
Simple, clean and well kept, located in a lively district. The amenities are basic but the location is very convenient.

Colonial House Inn (A)
318 W 22nd Street
(at 9th Ave.)
☎ 243 96 69
𝐅 633 16 12
A charming old house with a mainly gay clientele located in the heart of Chelsea.

The Gershwin (A)
7 E 27th Street
(at 5th Ave.)
☎ 545 80 00
𝐅 684 55 46
A youth hostel atmosphere (as well as rooms, there are dormitories for 4 or 8 people). Pleasant but not very quiet.

Hotel 17 (A)
225 E 17th Street
(at 2nd Ave.)
☎ 475 28 45
𝐅 677 81 78
www.hotel17.citysearch.
com
email: hotel17@worldnet.
att.net

A small European-style hotel with 120 rooms.

Howard Johnson (A)
429 Park Avenue South
☎ 532 48 60
𝐅 545 97 27
A modern, centrally-located hotel. Inexpensive but lacking charm.

Martha Washington (A)
30 E 30th Street
(at Park Ave. South)
☎ 689 19 00
𝐅 689 00 23
A hotel reserved just for women, which has a warm, homely atmosphere.

Standford Hotel (A)
43 W 32nd Street
(at 6th Ave.)
☎ 563 15 00
𝐅 643 01 57
A small hotel near the Empire State Building and Madison Square Garden.

Chelsea Hotel (B)
222 W 23rd Street
(at 8th Ave.)
☎ 243 37 00
𝐅 675 55 31
www.hotelchelsea.com
A legendary hotel, now slightly dilapidated, where the great names of literature and show business have stayed.

Doral Court (B)
130 E 38th Street
(at Lexington Ave.)
☎ 685 11 00
𝐅 889 02 87
A hotel with a European atmosphere a little away from the tourist attractions.

Doral Park Avenue (B)
70 Park Avenue
(at 38th St.)
☎ 973 25 00
𝐅 779 01 48
www.doralparkavenue
hotel.com
A fine Park Avenue establishment with a nice, original decor.

Hotel Metro (B)
45 W 35th Street
(at 6th Ave.)
☎ 947 25 00
𝐅 279 13 10
A classy, boutique-style hotel near Macy's, Madison Square

Garden and the Empire State Building. The rooms are fairly large and stylish and there's a good view from the terrace.

Jolly Madison Tower (B)
22 E 38th Street
(at 5th Ave.)
☎ 802 06 00
📠 447 07 47
A simple hotel with small well-kept rooms. The only branch of this Italian-owned hotel chain in America.

Dumont Plaza Hotel (C)
150 E 34th Street
(at Lexington Ave.)
☎ 320 80 50
📠 889 88 56
All the rooms of this hotel (studios or suites) have their own kitchen. A home away from home.

The Inn at Irving Place (C)
56 Irving Place
(at 17th St.)
☎ 533 46 00
📠 533 46 11
www.innatirving.com
Delightful, romantic and intimate, this hotel gives the impression of having gone back in time to the last century. Your own private brownstone.

Midtown (between 42nd and 58th St.)

Hotel Edison (A)
228 W 47th Street
(at Broadway)
☎ 840 50 00
📠 596 68 50
Small rooms that aren't ruinously expensive.

Park Savoy (A)
158 W 58th Street
(at 6th Ave.)
☎ 245 57 55
📠 765 06 68
A basic, budget hotel, very well located near Central Park.

Portland Square Hotel (A)
132 W 47th Street
(at 6th Ave.)
☎ 382 06 00
📠 382 06 84
Don't be put off by the pink lobby – the rooms are small, but adequate.

YMCA Vanderbilt Hotel (A)
224 E 47th Street
(at 2nd Ave.)
☎ 756 96 00
📠 752 02 10
The best youth hostel in New York for low budgets, equipped with a full fitness centre.

Ameritania (B)
230 W 54th Street
(at Broadway)
☎ 247 50 00
📠 247 33 13
A cool, contemporary hotel, near the Broadway theatres.

Fitzpatrick Manhattan Hotel (B)
687 Lexington Avenue
(at 56th St.)
☎ 355 01 00
📠 355 13 71
Irish charm, as its name implies, with 92 large, tasteful rooms and 52 suites.

Gorham Hotel (B)
136 W 55th Street
(at 7th Ave.)
☎ 245 18 00
📠 582 83 32
www.gorhamhotel.com
Spacious rooms with their own kitchenettes. Great for families.

Mansfield Hotel (B)
12 W 44th Street
(at 5th Ave.)
☎ 944 60 50
📠 764 44 77
A hotel with a Victorian decor and the air of an English club.

Quality Hotel Midtown (B)
59 W 46th Street
(at 6th Ave.)
☎ 719 23 00
📠 790 27 60
Comfortable and pleasantly decorated, located right in the centre of everything and not too expensive either.

Salisbury Hotel (B)
123 W 57th Street
(at 7th Ave.)
☎ 246 13 00
📠 977 77 52
www.nycsalisbury.com
Rooms with large wardrobes, safes and free breakfast. Choose a room at the back, or on an upper floor.

HOTELS

Wyndham Hotel (B)
42 W 58th Street
(at 5th Ave.)
☎ 753 35 00
☏ 754 56 38
A charming, comfortable hotel with 200 rooms.

Casablanca Hotel (C)
147 W 43rd Street
(at Broadway)
☎ 869 12 12
☏ 391 75 85
www.casablancahotel.com
As its name implies, a hotel with a Moroccan theme (decor and furniture) and good service.

**Doubletree
Guest Suites (C)**
1568 Broadway (at 47th St.)
☎ 719 16 00
☏ 403 64 30
A Times Square hotel with a Kids' Club, where children are really welcome.

**The Drake Swissotel
New York (C)**
440 Park Avenue
(at 56th St.)
☎ 421 09 00
☏ 371 41 90
24-hour room service, deluxe spa and fitness centre and large desks with fax machines. A great place if you're in town on business.

The Michelangelo (C)
152 W 51st Street
(at 7th Ave.)
☎ 765 05 05
☏ 581 76 18
www.michelangelohotel.com
Pleasant, comfortable rooms and an entrance that makes you feel like you're in Italy.

Le Parker-Meridien (C)
118 W 57th Street
(at 7th Ave.)
☎ 245 50 00
☏ 307 17 76
www.leparkermeridien.net
'Uptown not uptight' hotel with 730 spacious rooms with great views. Fitness centre and cocktail bar.

Waldorf-Astoria (C)
301 Park Avenue
(at 49th St.)
☎ 355 30 00

☏ 872 72 72
1,380 rooms, including 200 suites, each with original Art Deco motifs. All have marble bathrooms.

Warwick Hotel (C)
65 W 54th Street
(at 6th Ave.)
☎ 247 27 00
☏ 247 27 25
www.warwickhotelny.com
Built in 1926 and recently renovated, the Warwick has 422 fine, well-decorated rooms with marble bathrooms. One of New York's premier hotels.

Uptown (above 58th St.)

Hotel Beacon (A)
2130 Broadway
(at 75th St.)
☎ 787 11 00
☏ 724 08 39
A relaxed hotel near the Lincoln Center that offers large rooms with bathrooms and fully-equipped kitchenettes.

The Milburn (A)
242 W 76th Street
(at Broadway)
☎ 362 10 06
☏ 721 54 76
An eclectic, slightly kitsch decor but 111 spacious rooms with kitchenettes. Children under 12 stay free. Suite 106 is an unusual, tech-based art gallery.

West Side YMCA (A)
5 W 63rd Street
(Central Park West)
☎ 875 41 00
☏ 875 13 34
The largest YMCA in the world, housed in a landmark building just off Central park. For budget travellers wanting a great location who don't mind shared bathrooms.

The Excelsior (B)
45 W 81st Street
(Central Park West)
☎ 362 92 00
☏ 580 39 72
www,excelsiorhotelny.com
A 4-star landmark in New York's Upper West Side, near the Museum of Natural History and Central Park.

The Franklin (B)
164 E 87th Street
(at Lexington Ave.)
☎ 369 10 00
☏ 369 80 00
Tiny rooms but sophisticated, contemporary furniture.

The Mayflower (B)
15 Central Park West
(at 61st St.)
☎ 265 00 60
☏ 265 02 27
www.mayflowerhotel.com
A charming hotel with fine furniture overlooking Central Park.

The Lowell Hotel (C)
28 E 63rd Street
(at Madison Ave.)
☎ 838 14 00
☏ 319 42 30
Only 65 rooms and suites but one of the most luxurious and elegant hotels in the city.

The Plaza (C)
5th Avenue (at 59th St.)
☎ 759 30 00
☏ 759 31 67
www.fairmont.com
email: newyork@fairmont.com
One of the most famous hotels in New York. The very height of luxury and the 'crown jewel of Manhattan's fabled 5th Avenue'.

HOTELS

Restaurants are generally open from noon to 3pm for lunch and from 5.30 to 10.30pm for dinner (a little later on Friday and Saturday evenings). The letter in brackets after each restaurant indicates the price range for a 3-course meal (starter, main course and dessert), not including tax, tips and drinks but please note that these prices are only a guide:

A – under $25
B – $25-$40
C – $40-60
D – over $60

For more information see pp. 68-69.

Above Houston Street

Bistro Margot (A)
26 Prince Street
(at Mott St.)
☎ 274 10 27
A tiny place, but highly recommended for its succulent and inventive Sunday brunch.

Ghenet (A)
284 Mulberry Street
(at Prince St.)
☎ 343 18 88
A remarkable Ethiopian restaurant where you eat, according to tradition, with your fingers. Excellent value for money.

Johnny Rockets – the Original Hamburger (A)
42 E 8th Street
(at Greene St.)
☎ 253 81 75
A diner with a typical 1950s look – each table even has its own jukebox. A great place to try a real American hamburger and a milkshake.

Nyonya Cuisine Penang (A)
194 Grand Street
(at Mulberry St.)
☎ 343 67 01
In the very centre of Chinatown, a good restaurant serving delicious Malaysian cuisine.

Penang (A)
109 Spring Street
(at Greene St.)
☎ 274 88 83
You'll find a rich decor and refined Malaysian cuisine in this restaurant, situated in the heart of SoHo. The prices are quite affordable, which is unusual in this district. Often packed.

Petite Abeille (A)
134 West Broadway
(at Duane St.)
☎ 791 13 60
This Belgian chain of restaurants just keeps expanding in Manhattan. Open from 9am, you can enjoy food all day here, from a simple waffle to a full meal. Great beers.

Pão (A)
322 Spring Street
(at Greenwich St.)
☎ 334 54 64
Portuguese cuisine that's both traditional and contemporary. The bread and wine list are a plus.

Rice (A)
227 Mott Street
(at Spring St.)
☎ 226 57 75
A tiny, but very trendy spot, which serves rice in all it forms, from paella to sushi. A pan-Southeast-Asian-Indo-Carribean menu.

Sidewalk Café (A)
94 Avenue A (at 6th St.)
☎ 473 73 73
Open 24 hours a day, this place is unbeatable for its American brunch, which costs less than $8 and even includes champagne! The back room doubles as a music venue.

Blue Ribbon (B)
97 Sullivan Street
(at Spring St.)
☎ 274 04 04
Open to 4am, this restaurant serving American cuisine is one of the hottest addresses in SoHo. The steak tartare is excellent.

Café Habana (B)
17 Prince Street
(at Elizabeth St.)
☎ 625 20 01
This small restaurant looks more like a diner. It serves Cuban food and is very popular. You may have to wait.

Kitchen Club (B)
30 Prince Street
(at Mott St.)
☎ 274 00 25
A blend of Japanese and European cuisine in a restaurant of modest dimensions but enormous creativity.

Le Père Pinard (B)
175 Ludlow Street
(at Houston St.)
☎ 777 49 17
This restaurant, which is also a wine bar, serves a selection of dishes with the gentle flavours of Southern France.

Peasant (B)
194 Elizabeth Street
(at Prince St.)
☎ 965 95 11
This unusual Italian restaurant has a splendid decor. The meat is grilled over a huge wood fire. The lamb is to die for.

The Screening Room (B)
54 Varick Street
(at Laight St.)
☎ 334 21 00
The cuisine is inventive at this restaurant, which also serves as a cinema, located right in the heart of TriBeCa.

Tomoe Sushi (B)
172 Thomson Street
(at Houston St.)
☎ 777 93 46
There's always a queue for this sushi restaurant, which is one of the best you'll find in New York.

Casa La Femme (C)
150 Wooster St.
(at Prince St.)
☎ 505 00 05
An exotic setting (the SoHo version of a Bedouin tent) and good Egyptian dishes.

Montrachet (C)
239 West Broadway
☎ 219 27 77
Contemporary French cuisine in a classy but unpretentious restaurant.

The Odeon (C)
145 West Broadway
(at Thomas St.)
☎ 233 05 07
*Good Franco-American fare
in a brasserie that's been in
fashion for nearly twenty years.*

Torch (C)
134 Ludlow Street
(at Rivington St.)
☎ 228 51 51
*A warm atmosphere, live music
every evening (usually jazz)
and an excellent cuisine that's a
mix of French and South
American influences.*

Zoë (C)
90 Prince Street
(at Broadway)
☎ 966 67 22
*Sophisticated American food
in a pleasant restaurant with a
mixed clientele.*

Chanterelle (D)
2 Harrison Street
(at Hudson St.)
☎ 966 69 60
*Perfect French cuisine, New
York-style. One of the city's
culinary high spots, but very
expensive.*

Between Houston and 14th St.

Arturo's Pizzeria (A)
106 Houston Street
(at Thomson St.)
☎ 677 38 20
*Good pizzas, but it's mainly
the typical Greenwich Village
atmosphere that draws the
crowd of regulars.*

Decibel Sake Bar (A)
240 E 9th Street
(at 2nd Ave.)
☎ 979 27 33
*A tiny restaurant which fills up
very quickly. Above all noted for
its sake menu, but the cuisine is
just as good.*

Dojo (A)
24-26 St Marks Place
(at 2nd Ave.)
☎ 674 98 21
*A noisy establishment with an
alternative image befitting the
area, but the food is simple,
well-prepared and good value.*

Elvie's Turo-Turo (A)
214 1st Avenue
(at 12th St.)
☎ 473 77 85
*The city's best Filipino
restaurant, noted for its savoury
dishes and unbeatable prices
($5 for a huge meal with a
choice of two main dishes
and rice).*

Esashi (A)
32 Avenue A (at 2nd St.)
☎ 505 87 26
*In spite of its decor, which
resembles a canteen, this is
a great place for sushi.*

John's Pizzeria (A)
278 Bleecker Street
(at 7th Ave.)
☎ 243 16 80
*Even if the service leaves
something to be desired, you'll
be eating one of the finest
pizzas in New York here, with
crust as thin and crisp as you
could wish. There's much
debate as to whether it's the
best pizzeria in town.*

Kiev (A)
117 2nd Avenue
(at E 7th St.)
☎ 674 40 40
*Another city institution that's
always open, serving Eastern
European food.*

Moustache (A)
90 Bedford Street
(at Grove St.)
☎ 229 22 20
*Fresh, delicious Middle Eastern
cuisine served in a tiny setting.
Be patient, it's worth the wait.*

Thali (A)
28 Greenwich Avenue
(at Perry St.)
☎ 367 74 11
*Disappointing decor, fewer than
30 seats and no menu, but
fantastic and ridiculously cheap
vegetarian Indian cuisine
($9 for dinner and $6 for Thali
at lunchtime!).*

Veselka (A)
144 2nd Avenue
(at 9th St.)
☎ 228 96 82
*Solid, inexpensive Eastern
European fare, such as blinis
and potato pancakes. Always
packed, always open.*

RESTAURANTS

Dok Suni's (B)
119 1st Avenue
(at 7th St.)
☎ 477 95 06
Considered one of the best Korean restaurants in town, the cuisine is highly inventive and very refined.

Grove (B)
314 Bleecker Street
(at Grove St.)
☎ 675 94 63
American cuisine in a cosy setting perfect for dinner for two. Don't miss the pleasant garden in summer.

Home (B)
20 Cornelia Street
(at Bleecker St.)
☎ 243 95 79
Original US food in a country cottage setting.

Ike (B)
103 2nd Avenue
(at 6th St.)
☎ 388 03 88
This bar/restaurant offers excellent cuisine in a bright, ultra-modern decor. The brunch is simply divine. At weekends a DJ livens up the atmosphere in the evenings.

Le Zoo (B)
314 W 11th Street
(at Greenwich St.)
☎ 620 03 93
A small French restaurant in the heart of the West Village that's informal, inexpensive and serves inventive cuisine. What more could you want?

Lucky Cheng (B)
24 1st Avenue
(at 2nd St.)
☎ 473 05 16
Very fashionable despite the unremarkable Asian food. All the waiters and waitresses are transvestites.

Pisces (B)
95 Avenue A (at 6th St.)
☎ 260 66 60
Packed, noisy and frequented by the East Village crowd. Fabulous fish and seafood.

Pò (B)
31 Cornelia Street
(at Bleecker St.)
☎ 645 21 89
A very popular, romantic little restaurant serving Italian cuisine.

Restaurant Florent (B)
69 Gansevoort Street
(at Greenwich St.)
☎ 989 57 79
A French restaurant with a mixed clientele, bang in the heart of the meat markets. Open until 5am.

Roettele A.G. (B)
126 E 7th Street
(at 1st Ave.)
☎ 674 41 40
Swiss cuisine in a nice, kitsch setting.

Gotham Bar & Grill (C)
12 E 12th Street
(at 5th Ave.)
☎ 620 40 20
A fine, roomy setting, delicious American dishes and excellent presentation.

Between 14th St. and 42nd St.

Eighteenth & Eighth (A)
159 8th Avenue
(at 18th St.)
☎ 242 50 00
A friendly, gay atmosphere, good American food and very low prices.

Bright Food Shop (B)
216 8th Avenue
(at 21st St.)
☎ 243 44 33
A simply decorated diner serving American cuisine from the deep south. Quite spicy!

El Cid (B)
322 W 15th Street
(at 8th Ave.)
☎ 929 93 32
Delicious Spanish cuisine with over 30 varieties of tapas. Popular and noisy.

Markt (B)
401 W 14th Street
(at 9th Ave.)
☎ 727 33 14
Large, chic and trendy Belgian brasserie. Don't miss the noted moules-frites.

Old Homestead (B)
56 9th Avenue
(at 14th St.)
☎ 242 90 40
The oldest steakhouse in town, where the meat is succulent and prepared with finesse.

Patria (C)
250 Park Avenue South
(at 20th St.)
☎ 777 62 11
A fine, large restaurant serving Spanish nouvelle cuisine with a South American flavour.

Union Square Cafe (C)
21 E 16th Street
(at Union Square West)
☎ 243 40 20
Outstanding American cuisine in one of the best restaurants in New York. Book well in advance.

Verbena (C)
54 Irving Place
(at 17th St.)
☎ 260 54 54
Elegant and cosy. The chef opts for strong, original flavours.

Midtown (between 42nd St. and 58th St.)

Island Spice (A)
402 W 44th Street
(at 10th Ave.)
☎ 765 17 37
As the name suggests, you'll sample refined Caribbean (Jamaican in particular) cuisine here. Try the cocktails.

Lakruwana (A)
358 W 44th Street
(at 8th Ave.)
☎ 957 44 80
Delicate Sri Lankan cuisine that's very different from Indian food.

Rice'n'beans (A)
744 9th Avenue
(at 50th St.)
☎ 265 44 44
A tiny, welcoming restaurant serving good Brazilian cuisine. Huge portions.

Delta Grill (B)
700 9th Avenue
(at 48th St.)
☎ 956 09 34
An excellent place to try the delights of cajun food, straight from the streets of New Orleans. Live music every evening.

Ipanema (B)
13 W 46th Street
(at 5th Ave.)
☎ 730 58 48

Lots of style and exotic flavours in this restaurant serving Portuguese-Brazilian specialities.

An American Place (C)
Benjamin Hotel
565 Lexington Avenue
(at 50th St.)
☎ 888 56 50
A fine Art Deco restaurant serving excellent, creative American nouvelle cuisine.

Coco Pazzo Teatro (C)
224 W 49th Street
☎ 320 29 29
The height of fashion. A blend of Italian and Asian flavours and visually stunning dishes. Fantastic desserts.

Felidia (C)
243 E 58th Street
(at 3rd Ave.)
☎ 758 14 79
For many, the best Italian restaurant in New York. The pasta will bowl you over.

Le Bernardin (D)
155 W 51st Street
(at 6th Ave.)
☎ 489 15 15
If you like fish and seafood and are prepared to pay for it, don't hesitate.

Le Cirque 2000 (D)
New York Palace Hotel
455 Madison Avenue
(at 50th St.)
☎ 303 77 88
A place to see and be seen, where New York celebrities hang out.

Uptown
(above 58th St.)

Josie's (A)
300 Amsterdam Avenue
(at 74th St.)
☎ 769 12 12
Organic food is a speciality here – even the water used for cooking is multi-purified! Delicious dishes.

Boathouse Cafe (B)
Central Park
(at E 72nd St. level)
☎ 517 22 33
Located in Central Park and one of the nicest venues for a waterside lunch.

Josephina (B)
1900 Broadway
(at 63rd St.)
☎ 799 10 00
Close to the Lincoln Center, with a lovely, retro decor. American cuisine.

Metisse (B)
239 W 105th Street
(at Broadway)
☎ 666 88 25
Simple, perfect French cuisine in a slightly out-of-the-way restaurant. They serve delicious desserts.

Cafe Botanica (C)
Essex House
160 Central Park South
(at 6th Ave.)
☎ 484 51 20
Restful, elegant conservatory decor and cuisine from all over the world.

Etats Unis (C)
242 E 81st Street
(at 2nd Ave.)
☎ 517 88 26
It's only the name that's French in this restaurant, which serves American cuisine of the highest order. According to Time Out *magazine, it's one of the best restaurants in New York*

Jojo (C)
160 E 64th Street
(at 3rd Ave.)
☎ 223 56 56
Bistrot cuisine reinvented by one of the most talented chefs of the day. Simple and informal.

Jean-Georges (D)
Trump International Hotel and Tower
1 Central Park West
(at Columbus Circle)
☎ 299 39 00
The new temple of New York gastronomy.

RESTAURANTS

TEAROOMS

Anglers and Writers
420 Hudson Street
(at St Lukes Place)
☎ 675 08 10
This tearoom has a literary atmosphere. The ideal place to spend the afternoon reading.

The Astor Court, St Regis Hotel
2 E 55th Street
(at 5th Ave.)
☎ 339 67 19
A grandiose setting for an expensive, civilised tea ($30).

The Fellissimo Tearoom
10 W 56th Street
(at 5th Ave.)
☎ 956 00 82
Oriental luxury – Japan New York-style, housed in an Asian-themed department store.

Mark's Bar at the Mark Hotel
25 E 77th Street
(at 5th Ave.)
☎ 879 18 64
www.mandarinoriental.com
Open every day
noon–1am
With all the atmosphere of an English club.

The Museum Café, Guggenheim Museum
1071 5th Ave. (at 82nd St.)
☎ 427 56 82
Located inside the museum, with walls covered with photos of high points in its history.

Patisserie Claude
187 W 4th Street
(at Barrow St.)
☎ 255 59 11
Come here to try some delicious French pastries.

Sarabeth's Kitchen
1295 Madison Ave.
(at 92nd St.)
☎ 410 73 35
A true taste of New England. The weekend brunch is wonderful.

Tea and Sympathy
108 Greenwich Ave.
(at 8th Ave.)
☎ 807 83 29
A traditional English tearoom in the heart of Manhattan. The cream teas are divine.

The Tea Box at Takashimaya
693 5th Avenue
(at 55th St.)
☎ 350 01 00
A refined, Zen atmosphere in the basement of the department store. Huge choice of teas.

BARS WITH LIVE MUSIC

Birdland
315 W 44th Street
(at 9th Ave.)
☎ 581 30 80
www.birdlandjazz.com
Shows at 9pm and 11pm
daily.
Small and relaxed, a wonderful venue to listen to jazz. The great Charlie Parker called it the 'jazz corner of the world'.

The Bitter End
147 Bleecker Street
(between Thompson St. and La Guardia Pl.)
☎ 673 70 30
Rock, pop, funk – there's something for everyone at these evening music sessions.

C-Note
157 Avenue C (at 10th St.)
☎ 677 81 42
www.thecnote.com
Live music every evening (mostly jazz-funk), with a great atmosphere.

Cornelia St. Cafe
29 Cornelia Street
(at Bleecker St.)
☎ 989 93 19
A warm, romantic place to have a drink and listen to jazz in the heart of Greenwich Village. The upstairs restaurant is also superb, serving meals from $10-20.

Detour
349 E 13th Street
(at 1st Ave.)
☎ 533 62 12
A small, cosy bar, recognised as having the best jazz programme in town.

Izzy Bar
166 1st Avenue (between 10th and 11th St.)
☎ 288 04 44
A friendly bar in the East Village, where they essentially play jazz.

Lenox Lounge
288 Malcolm X Boulevard
(between 124th and 125th St.)
☎ 427 02 53
A legendary venue in Harlem for jazz – Billie Holiday was a regular here. When live acts aren't on the bill, a DJ spins a mix of reggae, disco and hip-hop. Open daily, noon to 4am.

Mercury Lounge
217 E Houston Street
(at Ave. A)
☎ 260 47 00
Listen to the best groups of the day in a cosy club.

Smalls
183 W 10th Street
☎ 929 75 65
www.smallsjazz.com
For real jazz fanatics – the musicians play all night long (until 8am!), seven days a week.

57-57, Four Seasons Hotel
57 E 57th Street
(at Madison Ave.)
☎ 758 57 57
Grandiose piano-bar-café with a sophisticated decor.

BARS

Around SoHo

Bar 89
89 Mercer Street
(at Spring St.)
☎ 274 09 89
A swanky bar serving good food and drink, with the most incredible restrooms in New York!

Bubble Lounge
228 West Broadway
(at White St.)
☎ 431 34 33
Chic champagne bar, SoHo-style.

La Linea
15 1st Avenue (at 1st St.)
☎ 777 15 71
A cool ambiance, excellent background music and a very smoky atmosphere.

288 Bar
288 Elizabeth Street
(at Houston St.)
☎ 260 50 45
A young, unpretentious crowd and the best barmen in town.

Around Greenwich Village

Blind Tiger Ale House
518 Hudson Street
(at 10th St.)
☎ 675 38 48
A vast selection of beers.

Drinkland
339 E 10th Street
(at Ave. A)
☎ 228 24 35
Unpretentious SoHo chic with a young, fashionable clientele.

Flamingo East
219 2nd Ave. (at 13th St.)
☎ 533 28 60
Several bars where the young in-crowd meet, with a terrace out front.

Grange Hall
50 Commerce Street
(at Barrow St.)
☎ 924 52 46
Pleasant decor and atmosphere in the heart of the West Village. Uma Thurman is a regular.

The Monster
80 Grove Street
(at Sheridan Square)
☎ 924 35 58
For over 10 years, this gay bar has welcomed a mixed crowd of all ages, races and sexes.

Niagara
112 Avenue A (at 7th St.)
☎ 420 95 17
A pleasant, sophisticated 1940s-style bar you mustn't miss.

Opium Den
29 E 3rd Street
(at 2nd Ave.)
☎ 505 73 44
A wide variety of music in a bar with a decidedly gothic decor.

Telephone Bar
149 2nd Ave. (at 10th St.)
☎ 529 50 00
A very comfortable pub with an English decor.

White Horse Tavern
567 Hudson Street
(at 11th St.)
☎ 989 39 56
One of the oldest bars in the city, opened in 1880. It was here that Dylan Thomas undertook the final drinking binge that killed him.

Between 14th St. and 42nd St.

Barracuda
275 W 22nd Street
(at 7th Ave.)
☎ 645 86 13
One of the best gay bars in New York. Excellent retro music.

Coffee Shop Bar
29 Union Square West
(at 16th St.)
☎ 243 79 69
Very, very trendy and packed, with a 1950s decor.

147
147 W 15th St. (at 6th Ave.)
☎ 929 50 00
A top bar full of 'beautiful people'. The counter is 10 m/30 ft long!

Midtown (42nd St. to 58th St.)

Flute
205 W 54th Street
(at 7th Ave.)
☎ 265 51 69
Simple, elegant and serene champagne bar – perfect for a romantic evening for two.

Hard Rock Cafe
221 W 57th Street
(at 7th Ave.)
☎ 459 93 20
The original theme restaurant. Large, noisy and more suitable for teenagers.

Jekyll & Hyde Club
1409 6th Ave. (at 58th St.)
☎ 541 95 05
This 'haunted mansion' has decor straight out of a horror film. Good fun, with plenty to entertain those with a ghoulish streak.

Mica Bar
252 E 51st Street
(at 3rd Ave.)
☎ 888 24 53
'Where the East meets the Eastside' – zen decor, friendly staff and delicious cocktails.

44 at the Royalton Hotel
44 W 44th Street (between 5th and 6th Ave.)
☎ 944 88 44
Very sophisticated theatrical restaurant in the lobby, designed by Philippe Starck.

BARS/CAFÉS

If you have a little more time to spend in New York, here are two walks that will take you beyond Manhattan.

A WALK TO BROOKLYN

The Borough of Brooklyn, which was attached to Manhattan in 1898, would now be the fourth largest city in the United States if it weren't part of New York. It has districts with an energy and charm all their own, a superb museum and parks.

To reach Brooklyn, cross the **Brooklyn Bridge**, which spans the East River. The 1km/½ mile long bridge, which is as famous as the Statue of Liberty, took 16 years to build and was completed in 1883. You can cross it on foot via a pedestrian walkway with views looking back towards Downtown (the entrance is on the level of City Hall). If you need a guide try **Big Apple Greeter** (☎ 669 81 59 www.bigapplegreeter.com see p. 33) and one of their team of volunteers will show you around. It's free, and they even pay for your Metrocard. If the walk gives you an appetite, stop off at the **River Cafe**, a barge moored just under the Brooklyn Bridge (1 Water Street, ☎ (718) 522 52 00, subway Clark St. or High St.-Brooklyn Bridge). In a romantic setting, you can sample some inventive American cuisine that's quite delicious, but unfortunately a little expensive, so you may prefer just to have a drink instead. Men are required to wear a jacket and booking is essential.

After your break, walk in the direction of Brooklyn Heights, which has the atmosphere of a Woody Allen film, with shady streets, three and four-storey houses, over half of which were built before 1860, and a marvellous view back towards Manhattan.

Art lovers won't feel left out. The **Brooklyn Museum of Art** (200, Eastern Parkway, ☎ (718) 638 50 00, www.brooklynart.org, subway Eastern Parkway-Brooklyn Museum) is one of the largest museums in the United States, with collections ranging from Antiquity to contemporary art. Its strong points are Egyptian art (only the museums of Cairo and London boast such rich collections) and the decorative arts, with twenty-eight reconstructed interiors. The absence of the crowds usually found in the Manhattan museums makes it a hidden gem. Next to the museum, the **Brooklyn Botanic Garden** (1000 Washington Avenue, at Caroll Street, ☎ (718) 623 72 00, www.bbg.org, closed Mon.) is home to over 12,000 varieties of plants and flowers, as well as a beautiful Japanese garden and an outstanding collection of bonsai trees. A celebrity path (with names engraved in the stones), pays homage to Brooklyn's famous sons and daughters, such as Barbra Streisand and Norman Mailer.

To end your day in Brooklyn, go and see a performance at the **Brooklyn Academy of Music** (30 Lafayette Avenue, ☎ (718) 636 41 00, www.bam.org, subway Atlantic Ave.-Pacific St.). It's a thriving urban arts centre that welcomes all that's new in the way of dance, music, theatre and opera. Robert Wilson, Philip Glass and Pina Baush regularly stage their new shows there.

A WALK TO HARLEM

For a long time, this district in the northern tip of Manhattan (above 110th Street) suffered from a bad reputation but things have improved in the last few years. You can now walk here quite safely in the daytime without fear of attack, but avoid the area after nightfall, and stick to the historical districts (125th Street, Lenox Avenue, etc). Alternatively, opt for a tour operator, who'll show you Harlem from the safety of a bus. **Harlem Spirituals** (☎ 391 09 00, see p. 116), a company specialising in tours of the district, offers a number of options. The best day to go to Harlem is Sunday. Start the day with the service at the **Abyssinian Baptist Church** (132 West 138th Street, subway 135th St.), the oldest black church in New York (see p. 66). The singing is wonderful, the families are all dressed in their Sunday best, and the atmosphere is quite unforgettable. Always bear in mind that you're in a place of worship and refrain from taking photos during the service.

Next try **Sylvia's** (328 Malcolm X Boulevard, ☎ 996 06 60, see p. 66), where you can sample the cuisine of the Deep South. Brunch after the service is a must. Harlem is also the district of jazz and there are many clubs. The **Apollo Theater** (253 W 125th Street, ☎ 531 53 05, see p. 67) is without a doubt the best-known venue. All the jazz greats have performed here, from Duke Ellington and Ella Fitzgerald to Billie Holiday, and it's still a showcase of new talent. The more intimate **Lenox Lounge** (288 Malcolm X Boulevard, ☎ 427 02 53, subway 124th St., see colour section p. X) offers a varied programme and is also a very pleasant place to go for a drink. The best way to get to one of these clubs in the evening is by taxi.

Conversion tables for clothes shopping

Women's sizes

Shirts/dresses

U.K	U.S.A	EUROPE
8	6	36
10	8	38
12	10	40
14	12	42
16	14	44
18	16	46

Sweaters

U.K	U.S.A	EUROPE
8	6	44
10	8	46
12	10	48
14	12	50
16	14	52

Shoes

U.K	U.S.A	EUROPE
3	5	36
4	6	37
5	7	38
6	8	39
7	9	40
8	10	41

Men's sizes

Shirts

U.K	U.S.A	EUROPE
14	14	36
$14^{1}/_{2}$	$14^{1}/_{2}$	37
15	15	38
$15^{1}/_{2}$	$15^{1}/_{2}$	39
16	16	41
$16^{1}/_{2}$	$16^{1}/_{2}$	42
17	17	43
$17^{1}/_{2}$	$17^{1}/_{2}$	44
18	18	46

Suits

U.K	U.S.A	EUROPE
36	36	46
38	38	48
40	40	50
42	42	52
44	44	54
46	46	56

Shoes

U.K	U.S.A	EUROPE
6	8	39
7	9	40
8	10	41
9	10.5	42
10	11	43
11	12	44
12	13	45

More useful conversions

1 centimetre	0.39 inches	1 inch	2.54 centimetres
1 metre	1.09 yards	1 yard	0.91 metres
1 kilometre	0.62 miles	1 mile	1. 61 kilometres
1 litre	1.76 pints	1 pint	0.57 litres
1 gram	0.035 ounces	1 ounce	28.35 grams
1 kilogram	2.2 pounds	1 pound	0.45 kilograms

A GREAT WEEKEND IN ...

Amsterdam	1 84202 145 1
Barcelona	0 54008 323 2
Berlin	1 84202 061 7
Brussels	1 84202 017 X
Budapest	0 54008 274 0
Dublin	1 84202 096 X
Florence	0 54008 322 4
Lisbon	1 84202 011 0
London	1 84202 168 0
Madrid	1 84202 095 1
Naples	1 84202 016 1
New York	0 54008 321 6
Paris	1 84202 001 3
Prague	1 84202 000 5
Rome	1 84202 169 9
Seville	0 54008 275 9
Venice	1 84202 018 8
Stockholm	0 54008 318 6
Vienna	1 84202 026 9

ROUTARD

Indulge your taste for travel with the ultimate food, drink and accommodation guides for the independent traveller.

Andalucia & Southern Spain	1 84202 028 5
Athens & the Greek Islands	1 84202 023 4
Belgium	1 84202 022 6
North Brittany	1 84202 020 X
California, Nevada & Arizona	1 84202 025 0
Canada	1 84202 031 5
Cuba	1 84202 062 5
Ireland	1 84202 024 2
Paris	1 84202 027 7
Provence & the Côte d'Azur	1 84202 019 6
Rome & Southern Italy	1 84202 021 8
Thailand	1 84202 029 3

VACANCES

Colourful, information-packed, leisure and activity guides. Hundreds of suggestions for things to do and sights to see.

Alsace	1 84202 167 2
The Ardèche	1 84202 161 3
The Basque Country	1 84202 159 1
Brittany	1 84202 007 2
Catalonia	1 84202 099 4
Corsica	1 84202 100 1
The Dordogne & Périgord	1 84202 098 6
French Alps	1 84202 166 4
Languedoc-Roussillon	1 84202 008 0
Normandy	1 84202 097 8
Poitou-Charentes	1 84202 009 9
Provence & the Côte d'Azur	1 84202 006 4
Pyrenees & Gascony	1 84202 015 3
South West France	1 84202 014 5